LOONS

Treasured Symbols of the North

TEXT & PHOTOGRAPHS BY WAYNE LYNCH

LOONS

Treasured Symbols of the North

Fitzhenry & Whiteside

Published in Canada by Fitzhenry & Whiteside Limited, 209 Wicksteed Avenue, Unit 51, Toronto, ON   M4G 0B1
Published in the United States by Fitzhenry & Whiteside Limited, 311 Washington Street, Brighton, MA 02135

Fitzhenry & Whiteside acknowledges with thanks the Canada Council for the Arts and the Ontario Arts
Council for their support of our publishing program. We acknowledge the financial support of the
Government of Canada through the Canada Book Fund (CBF) for our publishing activities.

ONTARIO ARTS COUNCIL
CONSEIL DES ARTS DE L'ONTARIO
an Ontario government agency
un organisme du gouvernement de l'Ontario

Canada Council   Conseil des arts
for the Arts   du Canada

Library and Archives Canada Cataloguing in Publication
Title: Loons : treasured symbols of the North / Wayne Lynch.
Names: Lynch, Wayne, author, photographer.
Description: Includes bibliographical references and index.
Identifiers: Canadiana 20220248818 | ISBN 9781554555734 (softcover)
Subjects: LCSH: Loons. | LCSH: Loons—Pictorial works. | LCGFT: Illustrated works.
Classification: LCC QL696.G33 L96 2022 | DDC 598.4/42—dc23

Publisher Cataloging-in-Publication Data (U.S.)
Names: Lynch, Wayne, author, photographer.
Title: Loons / author and photographer, Wayne Lynch..
Description: Toronto, Ontario : Fitzhenry & Whiteside, 2022. | Includes bibliography and index.
| Summary: "Acclaimed wildlife photographer, Wayne Lynch, focuses on the five species of loons
- the red-throated loon, the look-alike Pacific and Arctic loons, the familiar neck-laced common
loon and the yellow-billed loon, the largest and rarest member of the family. While the common
loon has been studied more than the other four species combined, this book will give a wider
scope and reach for all five species. A perfect book for those who live in loon country and want a
better understanding of the birds with which they live as well as for those who visit loon country
and are eager to interpret their wilderness experience. The book is also for those who may never
see a loon but who nonetheless want these birds to survive because they unfailingly fuel the
human imagination and spirit" -- Provided by publisher.
Identifiers: ISBN 978-1-55455-573-4 (paperback)
Subjects: LCSH Common loon. | Red-throated loon. | Yellow-billed loon. | Arctic loon. | Pacific
loon. |: BISAC: NATURE / Animals / Birds.
Classification: LCC QL696.G33L963L |DDC 598.442 – dc23

Edited by Carrie Love
Text and cover design by Tanya Montini
Printed in Hong Kong by Sheck Wah Tong Printing

Fitzhenry & Whiteside Limited

For Aubrey
The most fascinating person
I've ever known

Table of Contents

PLATE CCCVI.

Great Northern Diver or Loon.
COLYMBUS GLACIALIS. L.
Adult 1. Young in Winter 2.

CHAPTER 1

The Evolution of "Loon-acy"

I was ten years old when I got my first book about birds. It was a picture book showcasing roughly a hundred different birds selected from the 435 species painted in the early 1800s by the famous American naturalist/artist John James Audubon. As a ten-year-old nascent birdwatcher, I could only identify about half a dozen different birds, and that unimpressive list included the familiar barnyard pigeon, the cheerful, singing American robin, the ubiquitous urban house sparrow, and the noisy Canada goose. My treasured Audubon book featured not one of those birds but, instead, others, such as the Carolina parakeet, Eskimo curlew, great auk, passenger pigeon, and ivory-billed woodpecker, all of which were extinct. The book also included the colourful roseate spoonbill, majestic white gyrfalcons, flamboyant king eiders, and the endangered whooping crane, none of which could possibly be spotted near my home in southern Ontario. I was mystified as to why I wasn't able to find a single one of the birds contained in the book. I tried to memorize the evocative names of the different species, which included the purple gallinule, black skimmer, and barnacle goose. One of the exotics in my well-thumbed book was the great northern diver, which is known today in North

America as the common loon. The book's illustration was my introduction to this charismatic ruby-eyed waterbird with the distinctive checkered black-and-white plumage.

As a young schoolboy, I spent many hours wandering the woods alone hoping to see a secretive owl, an elusive weasel, a colourful beetle, or an iridescent dragonfly. It was the 1950s, and as a novice nature nerd I owned no binoculars or field guides, and I kept my interest in birds a secret to avoid the ridicule of my schoolyard friends. In those early years, I was never lucky enough to see a loon. It wasn't until I was in high school that I finally saw one for the first time. I was on a weekend camping trip with my family. On our first morning in the park, I snuck out of the tent early and sat alone beside a nearby lake. The sun was just beginning to break through the trees, and the water was shrouded in a silver mist. As I savoured the moment, a solitary loon swam out of the haze and wailed plaintively. The beauty of its call delighted me, and the primordial wildness of it filled my young heart with surprising joy. I was immediately smitten, and from that moment I have loved the loon like no other bird.

Some years later, while in medical school, I bought a cheap rangefinder camera from a classmate. I didn't know it at the

< *Opposite.* In July 1833, John James Audubon, the famous American naturalist and artist, painted the common loon in breeding plumage while in Labrador working in rain "that wouldn't stop." The winter plumage loon in the background was painted years earlier, in 1819.

time, but that purchase would eventually launch me on a forty-three-year career as a full-time freelance nature writer and wildlife photographer—a career I could never have dreamed up or predicted. But before that would happen, I would practise emergency medicine for a number of years and gradually hone my camera skills. One of my early photo fantasies was to make a canvas photo blind and use it to capture images of a nesting common loon in Quebec's La Vérendrye Wildlife Reserve, where I camped every summer and was lulled to sleep by the wild music of the resident loons. In early June 1974, that dream came true. With my homemade blind set in the water fifty metres (55 yd.) from the shoreline nest of a loon, I waited for the incubating bird to return to its duties. The chilly lake water came up to my waist, but a temporary soaking seemed a small price to pay for my photo plan to succeed. Soon, and with little warning, a loon surfaced beside the nest and quickly mounted it. My heart was beating so loudly with excitement I was worried it might frighten the bird away. My photos that day were not very good, but the thrill of the quest was energizing. My plan had paid off, and I was now a certified loon junkie. In the decades that followed that momentous June encounter nearly fifty years ago,

I have gone on to observe and photograph all five of the world's elegantly feathered loon species—from red-throated loons on Canada's Ellesmere Island at 82° north, to black-throated divers in Sweden, and yellow-billed loons in remote Siberia. I've spent dozens of hours huddled in photo blinds watching secretive Pacific loons nesting near Hudson Bay, where hundreds of hungry polar bears loaf on the shore throughout the summer. Most of all, I've worked with common loons, pursuing them from the forested hinterlands of Alaska and British Columbia to the warm coastal lagoons of Mexico's Baja California, where they winter with mother grey whales and their newborn calves. My life as a "loon-atic" has been unimaginably rewarding and pleasurably unplanned. I would do it all again in a heartbeat.

Humans are incurable storytellers. For millennia, our imaginative ancestors huddled around campfires in the darkness entertaining each other with tales about the wild creatures with whom they shared their world. The stories often changed, embellished and modified to enliven the narrative and lessen the tedium that comes with repetition. For the Indigenous Peoples of the tundra and northern forests, the loon was the predictable subject of countless traditional stories. The

< *Opposite.* If a pair of common loons become separated at night, they may wail mournfully at sunrise to help them reunite.

haunting nocturnal calls of the common loon were thought by the Cree to be the voices of slain warriors calling back to the land of the living. In the Shetland Islands, people believed that the plaintive calls of red-throated loons, locally known as rain geese, warned of a coming storm.

Every culture has a story of how the world began. Loons, which can dive and disappear with scarcely a ripple, were a predictably important character in many of these tales. In one such story from eastern Siberia, the Mother Goddess asks the yellow-billed loon to dive repeatedly as deep as it could to gather mud from the ocean bottom, one beakful at a time, and pile it up to build dry land where the people could live. In North America, Indigenous Peoples have similar creation stories. In one version of the world's beginning, the loon finally succeeds only after the otter, muskrat, and beaver have all tried and failed. In a different creation story, the Great Spirit is so happy with the landscaping efforts of the loon that he rewards the hardworking bird with a necklace of precious shells that magically transform into the distinctive feathers that adorn the loon's neck.

Loons also figured in the societal structure of some Indigenous groups. The Anishinaabe (Ojibway) First Nation, which once occupied the forested lands surrounding Lake Superior, originally structured their hunter-gatherer society around a system of grand families, or clans, of which there were six major ones: the Sandhill Crane Clan, Black Bear Clan, Wolf Clan, Pine Marten Clan, Moose Clan, and Loon Clan, each with its own spirit totem animal. In 1885, William Warren, who was born and lived among the Anishinaabe for much of his life, wrote *History of the Ojibways, Based upon Traditions and Oral Statements*. According to Warren, for a time the Loon Clan asserted that they were the heavenly ordained royal family of the Anishinaabe Nation. They pointed to the distinctive feather pattern on the loon's neck that was similar to the necklace worn by a chief; to them, this was ample proof of the clan's royal heritage. Not surprisingly, the other clans soundly rejected the Loon Clan's claim of regal status. Nonetheless, for all Anishinaabe, the loon was still a wild creature to be admired and emulated. If a warrior displayed extreme bravery in battle, he was described as being "loon-hearted," much as a fearless person might be described as "lion-hearted."

For many Indigenous Peoples, loons were not just important characters in traditional stories, they were also a

valued part of their diet. Even today, on the North Slope of Alaska, the yellow-billed loon is considered a delicacy. In the 1990s, I travelled with an Inuvialuit hunter and his wife on southern Banks Island in the western Canadian Arctic. When a yellow-billed loon accidentally drowned in a fishing net that was set for Arctic char, the bird was a welcome addition to the dinner pot. In 2007, roughly 1,000 yellow-billed loons were killed by hunters in the Bering Sea. In the same area in 2011, 151 loons were shot as part of the annual traditional harvest on St. Lawrence Island. A year later, 179 loons were killed. In both years, four different species of loons were included in those that were shot and eaten. More recently, in the summer of 2021, on Victoria Island, Nunavut, the two eggs in a yellow-billed loon nest I was excitedly monitoring were harvested by a hungry, sharp-eyed local on an ATV. I was told that the edible eggs were highly valued because of their large size.

Over the centuries, while loons were often celebrated and sometimes consumed, their soft, dense, patterned plumage was

∧ *Above.* The yellow-billed loon is arguably the largest of the five species of loons, and also the rarest. In Eurasia, the bird is known as the white-billed diver, and on the Chukotka Peninsula of eastern Siberia, it is known in the local language as the "walrus-toothed bird."

frequently used to make clothing. Traditionally, Indigenous Peoples in northern Alaska and Arctic Canada used loon skins to make indoor parkas that were lightweight and waterproof. One such parka, currently in the collections of the Royal Alberta Museum in Edmonton, was made from the head and neck feathers of several dozen common loons. The parka was sewn with sinew, and the cuffs and collar were trimmed with caribou and wolf fur. In the 1980s, in western Greenland, archaeologists found the mummified body of an Inuit woman buried in a boulder-covered grave. She was wearing an inner coat made from the feathered skins of red-throated loons and waterfowl. Archaeologists estimated that the woman died in the 1400s.

In the late 1800s, Indigenous Peoples in North America were not the only people to target loons. The so-called American sportsmen of the day also hunted loons—not for survival but merely as a puerile form of entertainment. In 1919, ornithologist Arthur Cleveland Bent described one such spectacle in Massachusetts.

[The common loon's] diving ability in dodging at the flash of a gun is well known. I once saw a remarkable exhibition of this power by a loon that was surrounded by gunners in a small cove on the Taunton River. There were six or eight men, armed with breechloading guns on both sides of the cove and on a railroad bridge across it, all within short range. I should not dare to say for how long a time the loon succeeded in dodging their well-directed shots, or how many cartridges were wasted before the poor bird succumbed from sheer exhaustion; but it was an almost incredible record.

Even today, more than a century later, loons are still occasionally shot for target practice and by frustrated anglers who see the birds as competitors.

In the last fifty years, humankind has slowly shifted its sentiments in favour of loons. The call of the loon, like the howl of the wolf, has the power to transport our minds and hearts to an ancient past when the environment and its creatures were favourably woven into the fabric of our humanity. As Walter John Breckenridge put it, the loon "puts the stamp of genuineness on a North Country setting like 'Sterling' does on silver."

Today, I am just one of thousands of Canadian "loon-atics," inadvertently encouraged, in part, by the government. In 1987, the Royal Canadian Mint replaced its crumpled, green one-dollar banknote with a gold-coloured coin featuring a portrait of Queen Elizabeth II on one side of the coin and a common loon on the other. The shiny coin soon acquired the popular nickname "loonie." Six years after the launch of the loonie, a pair of common loons was featured on Canada's twenty-dollar banknote, and these charismatic waterbirds retained their prominent position until 2004. During those same years, Ontario—Canada's most populous province—officially adopted the common loon as its provincial bird. It's hard to deny that Canadians really like loons.

South of the border, a multitude of Americans share our affection for loons. In 1961, Minnesota chose the common loon as its official state bird. In recent years, thousands of citizen volunteers in Minnesota, New Hampshire, Maine, Vermont, and New York State, known locally as "Loon Rangers," rescue trapped and injured loons. They tirelessly count and monitor local populations, build floating nesting platforms, and install signs and protective barriers around shoreline nests to alert the public to the birds' presence and the need to temporarily stay away. In New Hampshire, the Loon Preservation Committee (LPC) is particularly active in protecting these alluring, loquacious birds. In addition to the activities I just listed, the LPC holds an annual festival that includes an auction of loon paintings, photographs, and embroidered and woven goods. They also host a golf tournament, a kayak-a-thon playfully called "Yakking for

Above. To escape from danger, a common loon can quietly disappear within seconds, barely creating a ripple.

Above. The Canadian one-dollar coin, featuring a common loon, was first circulated in 1987 and quickly became known as the "loonie." A pair of common loons was featured on the country's twenty-dollar banknote from 1993 to 2004.

Above. In 2020, 32 percent of the common loon chicks in New Hampshire hatched on rafts installed by the Loon Preservation Committee—a testament to their effectiveness. The recent addition of UV-blocking shade fabric to cover the rafts reduces the high temperatures incubating birds must sometimes endure. During the July heat wave of 2018, ambient temperatures were 5.3°C (9.5°F) cooler under shaded rafts.

Opposite left. After preening, this Pacific loon raised itself out of the water as high as it could and flapped its wings repeatedly to rearrange its feathers—a common sequence in all species of loons.

Opposite right. The red-throated loon, the smallest and lightest of all the loons, breeds throughout the circumpolar Arctic, up to 83° north—the highest latitude of any species of loon.

Loons," a seven-mile competitive swim on Squam Lake, and a "Dunk the Biologist" event in which local researchers get wet for a loony cause. All of the activities raise much-needed money for the committee's conservation efforts. One of the most successful LPC ventures has been their loon webcams—two remote video cameras that continually stream on the internet the minute-by-minute challenges of two pairs of nesting common loons. In 2018, the webcams were viewed by loon enthusiasts in every state of the union and in a remarkable 184 countries!

Going hand in hand with the enhanced interest in loon conservation has been the scientific study of the species. The common loon is now perhaps one of the most studied nongame birds in North America. According to wildlife veterinarian and biologist Nina Schoch, there are two good reasons to study all the species in the loon family. The birds feed high on the food chain and can thus yield valuable insight into the pathways and deleterious impact of environmental pollutants. Also, because loons are strongly territorial and long-lived birds, with lifespans sometimes reaching thirty years, known individuals can be followed for many years, making them important long-term biological indicators of environmental health and trends.

This is a book about all five species of loons in the family Gaviidae: the red-throated loon (*Gavia stellata*), the smallest of the loons; the look-alike Pacific and Arctic loons (*Gavia pacifica* and *Gavia arctica*, respectively); the familiar neck-laced common loon (*Gavia immer*); and the yellow-billed loon (*Gavia adamsii*), the largest and rarest member of the family. While the common loon has been studied more than the other four species combined, I have tried to incorporate as many of the published research discoveries as possible on all of the loons to give the book a wider scope and appeal. Although I hope biologists and researchers will find value in this book, I have written it for those who live in loon country and want a better understanding of the birds with which they live, and for those who visit loon country and are eager to interpret their wilderness experience. This book is also for those who may never see a loon but who nonetheless want these birds to survive because they unfailingly fuel the human imagination and spirit.

CHAPTER 2

The Basic Loon

Sometimes, as a photographer, I am in the right place at just the right time. The morning of May 15, 2020, was one of those times. For about fifteen minutes, I had been watching an incubating common loon on an island nest about 100 metres (109 yd.) away. From where I was positioned on the edge of the lake, there was a cluster of cattails about fifteen metres (50 ft.) off to my left where I could see an American coot (a member of the rail family) huddling in the vegetation. The coot hadn't moved since I had first noticed it ten minutes earlier. It wasn't feeding or preening, so I thought it might be sitting on a nest. As I watched, the incubating loon's partner surfaced half a dozen times in front of the cattails where the coot was sheltering. Each time, the loon was hunched low in the water with its body partially submerged and its neck outstretched. I thought the loon was displaying mild aggression towards me rather than towards the coot crouching in the cattails. After a few minutes, the loon disappeared and the coot cautiously swam out from its hiding place. I swung my camera around to take a few photos of the swimming coot when the water suddenly erupted from a violent underwater attack by the highly aggressive loon. The terrified coot raced across the surface to escape but could not outdistance the enraged

loon. The attack lasted less than two minutes. It appeared that the loon eventually killed the coot with a lethal stab to the bird's chest. With the dead coot still floating in the water, the murderous loon did a triumphant "penguin display" in which it reared up in the water with its wings partially spread, then flapped several times to rearrange its dishevelled plumage, and swam back towards its incubating partner.

The scientific literature contains many reports of attacks by the different loon species on various kinds of waterfowl, but in most instances the aggression is limited to chasing and harassing. Especially pugnacious loons, however, have been reported killing adult common goldeneye, redhead, and ring-necked ducks. I will discuss this sinister behaviour in more detail in Chapter 6. For now, I want to focus on the different physical characteristics of loons, including their potentially lethal beaks, that make them the birds that they are.

EOCENE ORIGINS

The story begins with a predatory bird called *Hesperornis* (meaning western bird) that lived during the Late Cretaceous period, roughly 80 million years ago, when dinosaurs still roamed

< *Opposite.* This common loon stalked and chased an American coot and stabbed it to death in an attack that lasted less than two minutes.

and ruled the planet. *Hesperornis* was a large loon-like diving bird with small vestigial wings, large lobbed feet, and a long, pointed bill studded with rows of sharp teeth. Early taxonomists (the scientists who name and classify organisms) originally categorized animals and birds based primarily on the characteristics of their skeletons. They assumed that if two organisms had similar skeletons, they must be closely related to each other. The skeleton of a loon, minus the toothy weaponry, looks very similar to that of *Hesperornis*, so not surprisingly, taxonomists thought the two avian groups were closely related, and that modern loons were the living descendants of *Hesperornis*. Because of this perceived relatedness, loons, until very recently, were thought to be an

ancient family, which is the reason they were always featured first in any bird encyclopedia or field guide. For example, in the 2000 edition of Sibley's authoritative field guide to North American birds, loons were still placed at the beginning of the book.

In the early 1900s, loons were thought to be related to auks and grebes. All eat fish and aquatic invertebrates, capture prey with extended dives, and have their legs situated far to the rear of their bodies. Because of this last characteristic, the three were lumped into a single order, Pygopodes, meaning "rump-legged." Loons and grebes are similar in many other ways. Both need to run across the water for a distance to get enough speed to lift off, and both fly with their neck hunched down and their legs straight behind them. Because of the rearward position of their legs, both loons and grebes have trouble walking and are clumsy on land, requiring that both species build their nests close to the water's edge. Additionally, in many species of loons and grebes, chicks ride for safety and warmth on a parent's back in the early days after hatching. For all these reasons, the taxonomists of the day were boldly confident that the birds were closely related. What they didn't realize, however, was that different organisms responding to similar environmental pressures may end up evolving to look and behave the same, even though they are not related at all. Biologists call this fascinating process *convergent evolution*. Loons and grebes are a classic example of this. Other avian examples of convergent evolution include (1) carrion-feeding New World vultures and Old World vultures, (2) showy-beaked toucans in the Americas and hornbills in Africa and Asia, and (3) nectar-feeding sunbirds in Asia and Africa and sugar-sipping hummingbirds in the Americas. All look and behave similarly but none is closely related to each other.

It took the relatively recent introduction of DNA analysis to finally solve the mystery of bird relatedness. It turns out that loons are most closely related to penguins and albatrosses; grebes share a close relationship with flamingos, those filter-feeding, long-legged, pink beauties of the tropics. Loons, once thought to be an ancient species, are in fact a more modern radiation of birds. The most ancient bird groups are the waterfowl and chicken-like grouse and pheasants.

The oldest known loon fossils date from the later part of the Eocene era, roughly 37 million years ago. Around 21 million years ago, the ancestors of the present-day red-throated loon were the first to branch off from the main line of loon evolution.

The forerunners of the closely related Pacific and Arctic loons split off roughly 6.5 million years ago, and those of the common and yellow-billed loons diverged 3.5 million years ago. Paleontologists believe that all five species of loons living today evolved in the last 2 to 3 million years. They speculate that the look-alike Pacific and Arctic loons split from each other, as did the similar common and yellow-billed loons, during recent periods of glaciation when populations became separated and were isolated long enough to evolve into independent species.

BIG AND BEAUTIFUL

All of today's loon species are large birds, ranging in size from the lightweight red-throated loon, weighing 1.5 to 2.7 kilograms (3.3–6 lb.), to the heavier common and yellow-billed loons, weighing 3.5 to 6.4 kilograms (7.7–14 lb.). In the small red-throated loon, the male is typically 10 to 15 percent heavier than the female. The weight difference between males and females increases in the heavier species. In the common loon, males may be as much as 28 percent heavier than their female partners. Among researchers there is some lively disagreement as to whether the common loon, described in 1951 by British nature photographer G. K. Yeates as "a great battleship of a bird," is larger than the yellow-billed loon. The largest common loon ever weighed tipped the scales at a hefty 7.6 kilograms (16.7 lb.), but the weight of the species can vary by as much as 33 percent depending on whether the birds nest in the interior of North America or close to the coast, especially near the Atlantic coast where the heaviest common loons have been weighed. Although there has never been a yellow-billed loon that weighed as much as the heaviest common loon, I would argue that the more northerly ranging yellow-bill has a heavier average weight than the more southerly ranging common loon. As more yellow-bills are captured and studied, we may have a clearer picture of which of the two loons is actually the largest.

Because loons are such large birds and live out in the open on the surface of lakes and ponds during the summer nesting season, they are relatively easy to watch. This attribute undoubtedly contributes to their widespread popularity. If you are doubtful of this, try watching the comings and goings of a tiny sora rail as it furtively slips between the cluttered stalks of a cattail marsh— you will quickly come to appreciate the difference large size and visibility can make to a birdwatching experience.

Pure elegant beauty is another characteristic that makes loons the avian celebrities that they are. Within each species, the male and female have identical plumage, and all five species in breeding plumage feature distinctive, bold patterns in black, white, and grey, and in all but the red-throated loon, their feathers are embellished with patches of purple, blue, or green iridescence. The iridescence, a structural colour produced by the arrangement of the delicate barbules of the feathers, is a dynamic coloration that changes with the viewing angle, further contributing to the birds' visual allure.

Most biologists consider loons to be seabirds since all loons spend two to four years maturing on the ocean before they return for the first time to breed on freshwater lakes. After that, and for the rest of their life, most loons will spend roughly half of each year wintering on the ocean. Most species of seabirds, for example penguins, auks, albatrosses, cormorants, and frigatebirds, have the same plumage year-round, except for some changes in the colour of their face and beak. For example, in the familiar Atlantic puffin, the bird's facial feathers darken substantially in winter, and it loses the bright yellow coloration on its beak, but its wing and body plumage remain

> *Opposite.* As a consequence of convergent evolution, loons and grebes have many features in common: legs near the rear of the body that make it difficult for them to walk, young chicks that ride on their parents' backs in the early days after hatching, and robust pointed bills. Examples include: *(clockwise from upper left)* horned grebe, eared grebe, red-necked grebe, yellow-billed loon, common loon, and red-throated loon.

the same. Loons are different. In autumn, they replace most of their distinctive, handsome breeding plumage with bland, white and greyish-brown feathers that resemble the plumage of immature birds. The obvious question is, why do they do this? Biologists logically reason that such a drastic plumage change must be advantageous and confer some evolutionary benefit. Ornithologist Geoffrey Hill, in his fascinating book *Bird Coloration*, argues convincingly that the distinctive dark breeding plumage of loons is purposefully conspicuous and easily seen from a distance, perhaps to send a message that the owner is a healthy breeding adult and one prepared to defend its territory from rivals. In winter, when loons are not defending a territory and are often aggregating in feeding areas, their plain plumage may trigger less antagonism between group members.

The characteristic necklace in common and yellow-billed loons, and the white vertical striping on the neck of Pacific and Arctic loons, may be unique to each bird. This possibility is still being studied, but if proven correct, this plumage attribute would be helpful to researchers, who could use noninvasive techniques, such as photographs, to identify specific birds without the need to capture, stress, and band them.

All loon species may live twenty-five to thirty years, and like many birds with lengthy lifespans, loons do not reach sexual maturity or acquire full adult breeding plumage until they are several years old. In common loons, this does not happen until the bird is at least twenty-six months old. Biologists believe that the delay in plumage maturation benefits the young bird by lessening the likelihood that it will be confronted by aggressive reproductive adults who might otherwise view it as a challenger if its plumage was similar to the adult's. For a few years at least, the immature bird can concentrate on growth and survival rather than on avoiding needless clashes with cantankerous adults.

> ⌃ *Above.* An immature common loon retains a plain greyish-brown plumage until its third summer, when it finally moults into adult breeding plumage for the first time.

> ‹ *Opposite.* The finer the feather barbules, the closer the iridescence moves to the violet end of the colour spectrum. The plumage difference between the Pacific loon *(left)* and the common loon *(right)* is clearly visible.

^ *Above.* This male magnificent frigatebird has inflated his throat pouch to impress nearby females. Because of its 1.8-metre (6 ft.) wingspan and light body weight, the frigatebird holds the record for the lowest wing loading of any bird. The flamboyant male can float in the air for hours without flapping its wings a single time.

ON WINGS THAT WHISTLE

Ornithologist Arthur Cleveland Bent, in the colourful prose so characteristic of naturalist writers in the early 1900s, described the flight of the common loon: "The lines are perfect; the strong neck and breast, terminating in the long sharp bill, are outstretched to pierce the air like the keenest spear; the heavy body, tapering fore and aft, glides through the air with the least possible resistance; and the big feet, held close together and straight out behind, form an effective rudder. The power is applied by wings—which seem too small—driven at high speed by large and powerful muscles."

The ease with which a bird can take off, stay aloft, and safely land again is dependent on two main variables: its body weight and the surface area of its wings. All loons have a heavy body and relatively small wings, which impacts the nature of their flying ability. If you measure the body weight of any bird and divide that value by the surface area of its wings, you get its *wing loading*. The lower the wing-loading value, the more surface area there is to lift a unit of weight, and thus the easier it is for the bird to take off and fly.

The magnificent frigatebird of the tropics has the lowest wing loading of any bird, 0.34 grams per square centimetre. The wing loading in the ruffed grouse is 0.98 grams per square centimetre. In the horned grebe, it's 1.05, and in the hefty tundra swan, 1.43. Not surprisingly, all the loon species have high wing-loading values: 2.00 grams per square centimetre in the red-throated loon, 2.25 in the Pacific loon, 3.03 in the common loon, and 3.17 in the yellow-billed loon, earning the yellow-bill the dubious distinction of having the highest wing loading of any recorded bird. For loons, a high wing loading translates into too much body weight being lifted by too little wing area. The birds have one solution for this predicament—

they never let themselves be caught on a body of water where there isn't enough runway length to laboriously flap and sprint across the surface, great arcs of water spraying in their wake, to gain the needed speed for liftoff. They are like an overloaded cargo plane that needs a long runway. On a windless day, it may take a common or yellow-billed loon up to 400 metres (437 yd.) of strenuous effort to get aloft. The red-throated loon, which has a lower wing loading than the larger loon species, may be the possible exception to this need for a lengthy watery runway. There are old accounts of red-throats actually taking off from land. This fact has been repeated so often that it's no longer questioned, but I'm respectfully skeptical, as no recent researcher has ever seen this happen. Typically, the red-throat takes fifteen to forty metres (49–131 ft.) of water surface to become airborne. Red-throated loons can take off from much smaller lakes than the larger species; this ability gives them a competitive advantage in being able to occupy a greater range of wetlands, which in turn lets them nest farther north (up to 83° north in Greenland) than any other species of loon. In one study, a pair of red-throated loons successfully nested on a tiny lake west of Hudson Bay that was a mere thirty-four metres

(111 ft.) long and fifteen metres (49 ft.) wide. In blustery areas, strong winds can add lift for takeoffs, which may allow red-throated loons to nest on even smaller bodies of water. Along the windy northern shore of the St. Lawrence River, some red-throats have nested on offshore islands where the ponds were only 10 metres (33 ft.) long!

In forested environments, even after a loon has strenuously managed to become airborne, a loon's initial altitude may be too low to clear the treetops, forcing it to fly in ever-widening circles to gain the needed altitude. One pair of common loons I watched for several years in Alberta had to circle their small nesting lake three times to clear the tall spruce trees rimming the shoreline, even when a healthy wind was blowing.

Once aloft, a loon's flight is strong, swift, and direct, propelled by rapid wing beats. Researchers Åke and Ulla Norberg, studying red-throated loons in Sweden, calculated the wing-beat frequency to be 480 beats per minute when the birds first began to run across the water surface. It slowed slightly to 450 at liftoff and dropped to 360 during the climb away from the nesting lake. By comparison, the heftier common loon beats its wings in level flight at a somewhat slower rate of 240 times per minute. Compare this to the American crow's 120 wing beats per minute, the American robin's 138, the black-capped chickadee's 1,620, and the broad-tailed hummingbird's 3,000 per minute.

In flight, all loons beat their wings rather stiffly, moving them through a comparatively short arc. When relatively small and rapidly beating wings are keeping a heavy-bodied bird aloft, they generate turbulence and noise. Many times, when I have been tucked inside a photo blind with a limited view of my surroundings, I have been suddenly alerted to the return of a loon to its nesting lake simply by the whistling sound of its wings as it flew low overhead. Pioneer loon researchers Sigurd Olson and William Marshall, working in Minnesota in the late 1940s, claim the whistling wings of a common loon are audible up to ninety-one metres (300 ft.) away.

For many years, researchers tried to estimate the level flying speed of a common loon. The guesstimates ranged from 75 to 129 kilometres per hour (46 to 80 mph). Certainly, the most foolhardy attempt to determine a loon's flight speed was made in 1948 by pilot James Pittman, who chased a flying common loon with his small Piper Cub aircraft while flying north of Charlotte, North Carolina. To escape from its pursuer, the loon immediately went into a shallow dive, and despite the plane being at full throttle, Pittman was unable to match the bird's speed. The dubious experiment had to be halted after forty-five seconds, when a critically low altitude forced Pittman to prudently abandon the chase. After checking his airspeed indicator, Pittman concluded that "the true airspeed of this loon while being pursued was approximately 80 to 100 miles per hour." Today, modern radar instruments have calculated the flight speed of a common loon to be between 112 and 129 kilometres per hour (70 and 80 mph). With a tailwind, the bird's speed may increase to as much as 160 kilometres per hour (100 mph). The smaller red-throated, Pacific, and Arctic loons are thought to fly 20 to 30 kilometres (12 to 19 mi.) slower.

With such high wing-loading values, loons must fly rapidly or they would stall and fall out of the sky. To understand why this happens, it helps to compare the flight attributes of two types of modern aircraft: a glider and a fighter jet. The glider, with its large wings and relatively low body weight of around 500 kilograms (1,102 lb.), has a low wing-loading value, so it can fly very slowly and still stay aloft. By comparison, most modern

> *Opposite.* A common loon taking off is a splashy affair as the loon needs to vigorously flap its wings while running across the water—sometimes as far as 400 metres (437 yards), depending on the wind—before achieving lift off.

^ *Above.* During a landing, the common loon flares its webbed feet to slow its decent and help it to steer.

fighter jets are heavy (the F-15 weighs over 20,000 kilograms) and have relatively small wings to enhance their manoeuvrability, but because of their small wing area, they must maintain a high rate of speed. In many fighter jets, if their minimum airspeed dips below 320 kilometres per hour (200 mph), the jet stalls, loses lift, and drops, which is generally an undesirable situation. Think of a loon as an avian fighter jet that flies rapidly and maintains its speed with rapid, shallow wing beats.

Since the relatively small wing size of loons creates such flying challenges for them, why didn't they simply evolve larger wings? The most likely explanation is that larger wings would interfere with the streamlined, torpedo shape of the bird and hamper its manoeuvrability underwater. It was simply an evolutionary trade-off between flight performance and diving performance.

The recent miniaturization of instruments, combined with advances in satellite technology, have unlocked many seabird mysteries. For example, researchers in the Galápagos Islands not long ago discovered that great frigatebirds could stay aloft, flying at sea for up to two months at a time, without ever touching the water. These amazing seabirds sleep while flying, but very little—just forty-five minutes each night in short ten-second bursts. To do this, only one side of their brain sleeps at a time, leaving the other side awake to avoid splash landings, which would be lethal since they're unable to swim. As far as we know, no loon can sleep on the wing, so every loon that lifts off must eventually land, and their transition from air to water is nearly as exciting to watch as that from water to air. In their seminal monograph, *The Common Loon in Minnesota*, authors Olson and Marshall describe a typical landing: "The landing is a skillful, thrilling performance executed at high speed, necessary for the maintenance of control. The loon usually circles once or twice to lose altitude, or it may glide in directly at a steep angle. When ten to fifty feet above the water, the wings are set stiffly outstretched or in a sharp dihedral. In a

swift, smooth glide the loon executes a perfect seaplane landing, skimming low over the surface, dropping the feet slightly to contact the water and throwing a trail of spray for several yards as it slides into the water."

FOOT NOTES

The loon is a seabird that dives, and all diving birds propel themselves underwater in just one of two ways. They either paddle with their feet or flap their wings. Loons and cormorants are examples of foot-propelled divers, whereas penguins and auks are wing-propelled. If a bird wants to use its wings for flying as well as diving, it needs a low body weight and relatively small wings. I also discussed this evolutionary choice in the second edition of my book *Penguins of the World*. The thick-billed murre of the Arctic, weighing roughly 1 kilogram (2.2 lb.), is the heaviest of the auks and seems to be the critical size beyond which a bird cannot use its wings as both aerial

propellers and underwater paddles. At body weights greater than this, the increased surface area of the wings makes them cumbersome and ineffective underwater. One of two things can then happen: the bird can retain its wings for flying alone and use its feet to propel itself underwater—a strategy adopted by loons and cormorants—or it can abandon aerial flight altogether in favour of enhanced underwater flying. Penguins adopted the latter, and eventually evolved into very large flightless birds. One of the largest ancestral penguins, *Anthropornis nordenskjoeldi*, lived 40 million years ago. It stood 1.7 metres (5 ft. 7 in.) tall and possibly tipped the scales at nearly 135 kilograms (300 lb.). Legendary paleontologist George Gaylord Simpson quipped that "their height would not suffice for basketball, but their weight was about right for football." Today, the emperor is the largest surviving member of the penguin family and has a body weight that ranges from twenty-five to thirty-eight kilograms (55 to 84 lb.). The heaviest

Above. The heavyweight emperor penguin is the world's largest wing-propelled diving bird. Using its stiff flippers, the emperor can plunge to a depth of 564 metres (1,850 ft.) and stay submerged for up to twenty-eight minutes.

Opposite left. During a dive, a loon works its legs in tandem and sweeps them through a wide arc to propel it through the water.

emperor on record weighed forty-five kilograms (100 lb.), which is roughly the weight of a modern female Olympic gymnast.

All loons weigh over a kilogram, and some many times more than that. All of them need flight to migrate long distances between their freshwater nesting lakes and their wintering grounds on the ocean. Therefore, becoming flightless was never an option for loons. They rely instead on their feet for propulsion when diving, and big feet they have indeed. Loons have triangular-shaped webbed feet, which in an adult common loon may be thirteen centimetres (5 in.) long and eight centimetres (3 in.) wide. During a dive, loons kick both of their feet at the same time rather than alternately. This reduces the unwanted tendency of their body to roll from side to side. All foot-propelled divers alternate between brief bursts of forward propulsion followed by a gliding phase while they search for prey.

A loon has heavily muscled legs highly specialized for diving. Because its legs are located at the rear of its body, and oriented to the side, it can swing its legs through a wide arc (up to 80°) to generate the power and acceleration it needs when pursuing fast-swimming underwater prey. On the recovery stroke, its large webbed feet collapse and compress so that they cut through the water with a minimum of resistance. The bones of its lower legs are also greatly flattened, almost blade-like, to further lessen the resistance.

Water is 800 times denser than air and naturally resists the movement of any animal swimming through it. The extent of that resistance is related to the cross-sectional area of the animal's body. The sternum, or breastbone, in loons, as in most diving birds, is elongated with a relatively shallow keel. This makes the bird more torpedo-shaped and lessens its cross-sectional area, while at the same time providing a large attachment surface for the loon's hefty flight muscles.

The large webbing on a loon's foot helps the bird propel itself

underwater, but it can also be an unwanted source of heat loss. To counteract this, the peripheral arteries in a loon's leg, which bring warm, oxygenated blood from the heart to the feet, are closely encircled by a rich network of small veins carrying cool, deoxygenated blood back to the heart. The two types of blood vessels are so close together that some of the warmth in the arterial blood heats the returning venous blood, and as a result, the loon loses less body heat overall. Biologists call this fascinating vascular arrangement a *countercurrent heat exchange*. Additionally, the tissues of a loon's foot that receive the cooler blood are adapted to still function well in low temperatures, so the bird can safely swim in icy water without any risk of tissue injury.

When a loon is on the water, its feet are usually hidden from view. Even when it climbs onto a shoreline nest, it's still hard to get a good look at a loon's floppy footgear. Periodically, however, a swimming loon may raise one of its feet in the air, shake it vigorously, stow it in the dry feathers under a wing, and continue to swim with just one foot in the water. This noticeable behaviour, called *foot waggling*, has been studied in detail in the common loon by veteran researcher James Paruk. All of the loon species foot waggle, as do grebes and many

diving ducks. Paruk wondered whether the energetic foot shaking was a comfort movement to stretch the leg muscles, an action to remove dirt from muddy feet, a way to conserve body heat when a lake is cold, an attempt to cool off when the air temperature is high, or a combination of these. Over the course of two years, Paruk curiously spied on ten pairs of common loons hoping to answer these questions. He discovered that both adult males and females, as well as newly hatched chicks, sometimes just one week old, all spent about the same amount of time each day wagging their feet. None showed a preference for their right foot over their left, and 80 percent of the time, the foot flapping happened when the bird was either preening

^ *Above and following page.* Wing-propelled divers, such as penguins and auks, mainly forage in the open ocean. In contrast, foot-propelled divers, such as loons and cormorants, hunt primarily in freshwater lakes and along ocean coastlines. One reason for this is that the thick aquatic vegetation in many freshwater lakes, as well as the dense kelp forests along various coastlines, would hinder any bird trying to use its wings to dive; the plant-congested waters are much better-suited for foot-propulsion.

‹ *Opposite.* This parent common loon had just spent ten minutes preening, after which it vigorously shook its right foot numerous times before tucking it under a wing.

or resting, and most often within the first hour after sunrise. Environmental factors, such as water and air temperature, had no impact on the conspicuous behaviour, although heightened wind speed and waves lessened its occurrence. It seems that when the wind is blowing strongly, a loon loses the ability to steer with only one foot underwater. In the end, Paruk concluded that foot waggling was mainly a comfort movement to stretch the loon's leg muscles, but it might still play a minor role in the heat balance of some individuals.

A MULTITASKING TOOL

An imaginative author once described the beak on a bird as the avian version of a Swiss Army knife. Birds use their beak to probe for food, kill prey, tear meals apart, defend against predators, fight with rivals, court a mate, build a nest, feed their young, and preen their feathers.

All loons have a narrow, strong, sharply pointed beak well suited for catching fish. The beaks of the Arctic, Pacific, and common loons are straight, but in the yellow-bill and red-throat they angle slightly upwards. Naturally, the bills of the smaller species are not as robust as those of the larger ones, and the maximum length varies markedly. The beak of the yellow-billed loon can be up to 9.7 centimetres (3.8 in.) long; the common loon, 8.8 centimetres (3.5 in.); the Arctic and Pacific loons, 6.8 centimetres (2.7 in.); and the red-throated loon, 5.7 centimetres (2.3 in.). In all loon species, bills do not reach full adult size until the birds are roughly a year old, and male beaks are usually a smidge larger than those of females, although the difference is almost impossible to detect in the field.

Loons differ from the majority of seabirds in not having a hook on the end of their bills. If you look back at the photograph of the frigatebird earlier in this chapter, you can see just how large the hook can sometimes be. Birds use the hook on their beaks to tear open prey and rip off pieces they can swallow. Adult loons swallow their prey whole, and parents don't tear prey apart for their chicks, so they have no need for such a hook. A parent will sometimes bring a fish that is too large for its chick to swallow, and the well-intentioned adult ends up eating the meal itself. In one case, an adult Pacific loon brought a fifteen-centimetre (6 in.) long fish that was much too large for its two-day-old chick to handle. The parent finally ate the fish after offering the meal to the hungry youngster for over twenty minutes!

Loons, like all birds, have no teeth. Reflect for a moment on why this is so. You'll recall that 80 million years ago one group of birds in the genus *Hesperornis* had jaws studded with sharp teeth, but this avian branch went extinct at the close of the Cretaceous period. Until quite recently, the primary explanation given for the toothlessness in birds was that it was a beneficial adaptation for flight. After all, a mouth full of heavy teeth would shift a bird's centre of gravity forward and make it a less efficient flying machine. Thus, the teeth had to go, and the bones of the beak were filled with air spaces to further lessen its weight. This explanation was all fine until 2018 when two paleontologists, Tzu-Ruei Yang and Martin Sander, suggested a possible alternate explanation for toothlessness, or *edentulism*, in birds. Today, it is common knowledge that birds are merely feathered dinosaurs, and they arguably should be included in the class Reptilia rather than in their own separate grouping, class Aves. While studying dinosaur embryos, Yang and Sander discovered that when teeth are forming, the rate of embryo development markedly slows down. They hypothesized that tooth loss in birds was ultimately driven by the necessity for faster embryonic growth, which would reduce incubation

❯ *Top Right.* In a rapid sequence of convulsive gulps, this common loon took just a few seconds to swallow a twenty-centimetre (8 in.) trout, affording its scanty taste buds little time to evaluate the meal.

Bottom Right. A persistent wind ruffled the back feathers on this nesting red-throated loon, and it quickly rotated its position to make itself more comfortable.

time. The egg incubation stage in birds is a vulnerable phase of reproduction, and anything that gets chicks safely hatched and out of the nest more quickly benefits the species. It's this kind of gee-whiz science that energizes me and fuels my life.

SENSING THEIR WORLD

The sense organs in a bird gather and transmit information about the world around it, and a loon senses in the same way as a human, using smell, taste, touch, hearing, and vision. But avian sense organs often function differently from those in mammals, and in many ways, we know relatively little about them.

No one has studied smell, taste, or touch in any of the loon species. It has long been known that among the tube-nosed seabirds, close relatives of the loons, some have a good sense of smell and use it to target fish-oil slicks on the ocean, as well as to locate their nest burrows in crowded colonies, but such abilities seem lacking in loons. Nonetheless, it's assumed that all loons have some sensory cells in their nasal cavities, yet how much or how little they use their sense of smell is a mystery.

Taste is another sense that is poorly studied in birds. Most birds have a few hundred taste buds on the roof of their mouth

or at the back of their throat, but unlike mammals, they have none on their tongue. Since loons never chew their food, and always swallow it whole, they may have little need for taste.

Researchers assume that loons, like all birds, have touch receptors in their joints, muscles, skin, and feather follicles. These relay information about the unwanted ruffling of plumage, the overstretching of muscles and joints, and the temperature of exposed skin. Again, so little is known about this rich sensory world in loons that any further discussion would be pure speculation devoid of any facts.

Hearing and vision are the two most important senses in loons, as they are in all birds. Because loons have such a rich vocal repertoire, it's safe to assume that their hearing is acute, at least within the frequency range of their vocalizations. When considering the nature of hearing in a bird or mammal, there are three aspects to consider: the frequency range of detectable sounds (measured in cycles per second, or hertz), the minimum threshold or loudness of a sound that can be perceived (measured in decibels), and the ability to determine the direction from which a sound originates and pinpoint its location.

When it comes to frequency range, no creatures can match the ability of mammals. Human hearing spans a range from roughly 20 to 20,000 hertz. This is the maximum range experienced by a young child. As we age, we slowly lose the ability to detect high frequencies, and our hearing range gradually shrinks. These numbers are important to remember only because it allows us to compare human hearing with that of other vertebrates.

As far as we know, bats, toothed cetaceans, and some rodents can detect the highest frequency range of any creature and are capable of producing and hearing ultrasounds (those above the frequency range that humans can hear) in the 80,000- to 100,000-hertz range. Some bats can hear frequencies as high as 210,000 hertz. Bats generate these high-frequency sounds and then listen for the echoes to determine the location and size of small flying insects.

In birds that have been tested, none of which were loons, the hearing frequency ranged from 30 to 10,000 hertz versus the 20 to 20,000 hertz of most young humans. No bird is known to hear frequencies higher than 12,000 hertz, and their hearing is most sensitive in the 1,000- to 5,000-hertz range. The majority of loon vocalizations fall within the 600- to 2,000-hertz frequency range.

The principal reason that birds have a narrower

hearing range than mammals rests in the anatomy of their inner ear—the fluid-filled portion of the ear where sound vibrations are converted into nerve impulses. In mammals, including humans, the sound-sensing organ of the inner ear is called the cochlea, because of its resemblance to the spiral shell of a snail. The spiral shape allows a greater length of receptive tissue to be packed into a small space. In birds, the sound-sensing organ is also called the cochlea, although it is a straight tube and not a spiral. Along the inside wall of the cochlea in both birds and mammals there is a sensitive membrane stretched throughout the organ's length that is receptive to different frequencies. Mammals hear a greater range of frequencies than birds mainly because their cochlear membrane is roughly ten times longer.

The second aspect of hearing to consider in loons is their minimum auditory sensitivity, or the loudness of the faintest sound they can perceive. Because the hearing threshold in humans can be easily and thoroughly evaluated, it has become the standard used to measure the loudness of sounds. Thus, the exact point at which an average young adult can just detect a sound from silence is zero decibels. Rustling

leaves have a decibel rating of 15; normal conversation, 45; crowd noise, 60; a vacuum cleaner, 75; and a pneumatic drill, 90. The threshold of pain is reached at between 115 and 120 decibels. The minimum hearing threshold in loons is a complete unknown and awaits the curiosity of a tenacious graduate student. Nonetheless, on a cool, windless night, the wail of a common loon can be heard by a human observer several kilometres away, and it's assumed that it's detectable by a neighbouring loon as well.

The final aspect of hearing to consider is the ability of a loon to pinpoint the location of a sound. Recently, when I was in a photo blind watching an incubating common loon, I heard some faint rustling in the cattails along the shoreline about ten metres (30 ft.) away. Eventually, a baby muskrat stuck its head up and satisfied my curiosity. The loon I was watching never changed its behaviour and never gave any indication that it had also heard the noise. Did it hear the muskrat and simply ignore it, or was it deaf to the sounds?

The ability to localize a sound relies on two sources of auditory information: the difference in the loudness perceived by each ear and the time lag between when a sound reaches one ear as opposed to the other. Generally, when the loudness of a sound is the same in both ears, and there is no time difference between your right and left side, the sound is directly in front of you or directly behind you. This pinpoints the sound in the horizontal plane, and humans can do this with an accuracy of within one degree. But what about the vertical plane? If a sound is directly in front of you, is it located high or low? In this instance, human ears perform almost as well, and we can pinpoint the vertical position of a sound within roughly two degrees. The ability of a loon to localize a sound is regrettably another unstudied aspect of their biology. Despite our limited understanding of loons and their auditory world, vocalizations

are very important elements of their behaviour and this topic will be covered fully in Chapter 5.

However significant hearing is in the life of a loon, vision is clearly the loon's primary sensory tool. A deaf loon can still dive and catch prey, avoid predators and dangerous rivals, locate a mate, raise chicks, and migrate, whereas a blind loon would perish within days. Virtually nothing is known about vision in loons. To help me answer some questions, I recently read *Bird Senses: How and What Birds See, Hear, Smell, Taste, and Feel*, published in 2020 by Graham Martin, an emeritus professor at England's University of Birmingham. Martin has been studying the sensory ecology of birds for more than four decades, and many of the details he describes about vision in birds unquestionably applies to loons.

In all birds, three important variables influence the sensitivity of their vision to various light conditions: the size of their eyes, the density and type of photoreceptors in the retina at the back of each eye, and the diameter of their pupils, which controls the amount of light that reaches the retina.

The size of a bird's eyes dictates the size of the images projected onto the sensitive retina. The bigger the image the

> *Opposite.* For a parent common loon to feed a tiny dragonfly nymph to its chick is a testament to the bird's ability to see clearly underwater, where it must locate such small, cryptic invertebrates amid tangles of aquatic vegetation.

better. Owls, for example, have exceptionally large eyes for their body size. Those of an eastern screech owl weigh 7.4 grams (0.26 oz.), which amounts to roughly 4 percent of its total body weight. Compare that to a human eyeball, which weighs about thirty grams (1 oz.) and amounts to roughly 0.08 percent of our total body weight. An owl's large eyes are one of the adaptations that help it to navigate at night. The eyes of loons are not exceptionally large, and the birds don't seem to have evolved this beneficial night-vision adaptation.

The avian retina contains two kinds of light-sensitive photoreceptors: rods and cones. The rods are stimulated by low levels of light and generate shadowy, grey images of poor resolution. Cones, on the other hand, require high levels of light to be stimulated, but they produce sharp, coloured images. The human retina contains a dense mixture of both rods and cones, which gives us good colour vision in the daytime as well as surprisingly good nocturnal vision if we give our eyes time to adjust to the low levels of nighttime light. No researcher has microscopically examined the retina of a loon, but we can assume that loons also have a rich mixture of rods and cones, endowing them with acceptably sharp colour vision for the daytime as well as the sensitivity needed for hunting in the low light conditions underwater.

A bird's pupils control the width of the beam of light entering the front of its eyes, and thus they determine the brightness of the image striking the retina. In daylight, the pupil size in loons is exceptionally small. During a dive, a foraging loon often makes a rapid transition from bright sunlight to dim underwater light levels. Its pupils undoubtedly react by instantly dilating to let in as much light as possible, but in all vertebrates, the rods in the retina generally need some time to become responsive to reduced levels of light. The human eye, for example, requires thirty to forty-five minutes to become fully dark adapted, and it's reasonable to assume that birds may also have an obligatory time delay, albeit possibly shorter than in humans. Since loons commonly make dives lasting less than a minute or two, this doesn't seem to give their retinas much time to become optimally primed for the dim underwater light. Penguins are faced with a similar dilemma of rapidly changing light levels during a dive. Ecologist Graham Martin hypothesizes that penguins are able to cope with this because their eyes are preadapted and continually ready to operate in a low light situation without the impediment of a delay. They accomplish this by restricting their pupils to pinhole size while they are at the surface in the bright sunlight. Then, when they dive, their eyes are already dark adapted and primed to function in the lower light conditions underwater. Since loons also have pinhole pupils, it's tempting to suggest that the same ingenious adaptation may exist in them.

When a loon dives underwater, it not only faces lower levels of light but also the sudden need to focus its eyes in a liquid medium. In birds, as in humans, the two main focusing units in an eye are the curved cornea at the front of the eye and the lens. Underwater, the cornea, which now has fluid in front of it instead of air, suddenly loses its focusing ability. The eye must now rely solely on the lens to create a sharp image on the retina. This is achieved by increasing the curvature of the lens, technically known as *accommodation*. The human eye has a limited ability to accommodate compared to most diving birds, which are able to dramatically increase the curvature of their lenses, enabling them to focus underwater. (For those readers addicted to science trivia as much as I am, the accommodative power in diving birds ranges from fifty to eighty dioptres, which

is five to ten times higher than in humans.) As far as I know, no one has determined the accommodative power in loons, but I think it is safe to assume that it is high since they rely solely on their visual acuity to hunt effectively underwater. I have frequently seen a parent loon deliver a tiny dragonfly larva to its chicks after diving down and plucking the insect from underwater vegetation, a task that would definitely require the ability to focus on fine detail.

Although there is still much to learn about vision in loons, there is one feature of their eyes about which there is absolute certainty. It relates to the vibrant colour of their irises. All adult loons have beautiful blood-red eyes, and the birds' tiny pupils make their stunning irises all the more visible.

In water, the red end of the colour spectrum is quickly filtered out and disappears completely at depths below ten metres (30 ft.), making everything look blue the deeper you go. Underwater photographers try to regain some of this lost colour by using a red filter on their camera lens. Many authors have erroneously suggested that the reason a loon has red irises is to restore the red coloration filtered out by the water. As discussed above, it's the diameter of the pupil that is important

not the colour of the iris. Eye colour in birds varies greatly, from black and brown, to orange and yellow, to blue and green—and a multitude of colours in between. If a red iris were beneficial in seeing better in a deep dive, then you would think that the emperor penguin, the deepest-diving bird in the world, which swims to depths of 564 metres (1,850 ft.), would also have red eyes, but in fact, its eyes are dark chocolate brown.

Even though the red eye colour in an adult loon is not involved in vision, it still has an important role to play in loon biology. Martin writes in *Bird Senses*, "Eye color in birds is concerned with social behavior, signaling such things as age, sex, emotional states and general fitness." In loons, although there is no eye colour difference between males and females, young birds signal their immaturity by having dark brown eyes until they are at least one year old. Most immature loons remain on the ocean for several years before they start to breed, and in all of the species, the changes in eye colour is poorly documented. In fact, immature loons may not acquire the red eyes of breeding adults until they become sexually mature in their second or third summer.

It's interesting to consider whether eye colour in loons might indeed reflect general fitness. When an adult loon moults its breeding plumage in the autumn, the colour of its eyes fades somewhat and becomes brownish-red or dark brown rather than the vibrant blood red so characteristic of the breeding season. In most birds, the yellow and red coloration in their feathers and skin is produced by pigments, called *carotenoids*, which the birds acquire in their diet. When a bird's diet is deficient, or its physiology compromised by disease, the vibrancy of its coloration is affected and becomes an honest cue of declining health and vitality. Many studies support this connection.

The production of colour in the eyes of birds is different than in feathers, and it's the least understood aspect of coloration in birds. The red, yellow, and orange coloration in eyes is not produced by carotenoids but by a different class of pigments called *pterins*. Unlike carotenoids, pterins are manufactured in the body of the bird and not acquired from its diet. It's unknown if the production of these unique eye pigments is influenced by the bird's health as it is with carotenoids. If it is, then the redness of a loon's eyes might reflect its fitness, signalling to other loons its strength or weakness. The plot thickens and, hopefully, exciting discoveries lurk on the horizon.

< *Opposite.* Many birds other than loons have red eyes, including the horned grebe (*upper left*), purple gallinule (*upper right*), spotted towhee (*lower left*), and black-crowned night-heron (*lower right*). Notice that the horned grebe, a diving bird, has the tiniest pupils of the four. The grebe, like the loon, may rely on pinhole pupils to keep their eyes preadapted for the lower light conditions encountered underwater.

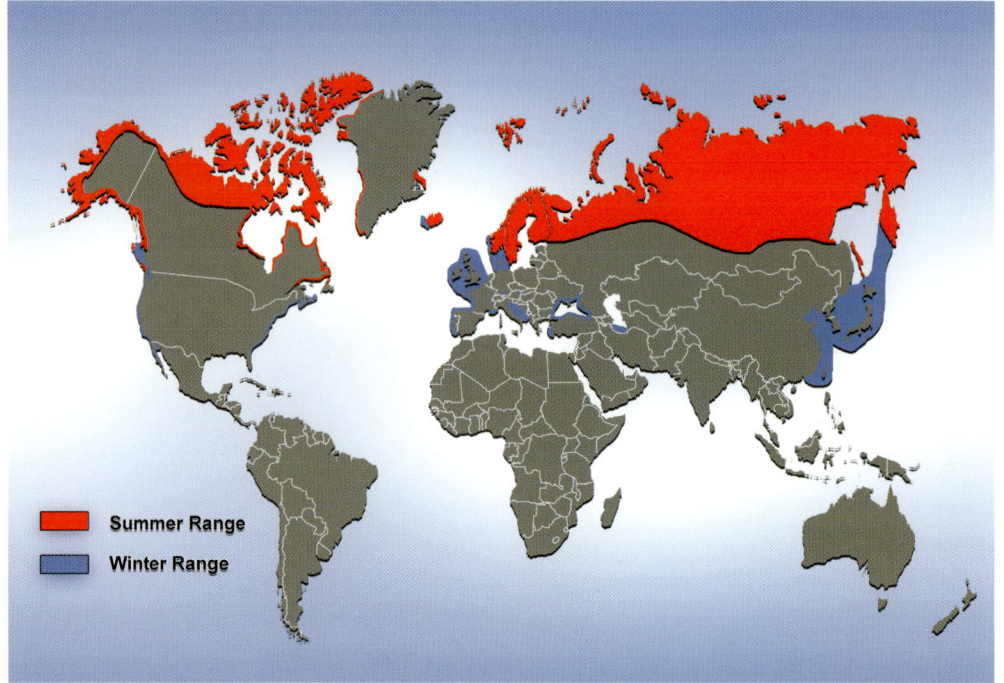

Summer Range

Winter Range

CHAPTER 3
Loons of the World

RED-THROATED LOON (NORTH AMERICA) /
RED-THROATED DIVER (EUROPE)
(French: Huart à gorge rousse)

Scientific Name: *Gavia stellata.* First described in 1763. The genus Gavia is derived from Latin for seabird or gull and was assigned by the German naturalist Johann Reinhold Forster during his around-the-world travels with Captain James Cook in the 1770s. The epithet *stellata* is Latin for "starry" and refers to the speckling on the bird's back in its nonbreeding winter plumage.

Field Identification: The smallest member of the loon family, although its size may overlap with some Pacific loons. In breeding plumage, it has a smoky grey head with a rusty throat patch, which often appears dark in flight. It has fine black-and-white vertical stripes on the back of its neck. Its underside is completely white and highly visible when the bird preens, flaps its wings, or flies overhead. When swimming, the red-throated loon tends to holds its head tilted slightly upwards.

Size: Weight is 1.3 to 2.3 kilograms (2.9–5 lb.) (30 percent smaller in Europe); length, 60 to 64 centimetres (23.6–25 in.); wingspan, 90 to 93 centimetres (35–37 in.).

Range: Breeds in the Arctic and boreal regions of the Northern Hemisphere, generally north of 50°. Winters along the Atlantic as far south as Florida and along the Pacific coast as far south as Mexico's Baja California. In Eurasia, it winters on the coast of Portugal, in the Mediterranean, in the Black and Caspian Seas, and on the coast of Asia as far south as Taiwan and southeast China.

Status: Global population is 200,000 to 600,000. Although the red-throat is declining, it remains designated as a species of Least Concern by the International Union for Conservation of Nature (IUCN) because of its large population size, vast range, and the slow rate of decline. The IUCN is a highly recognized global conservation organization headquartered in Switzerland.

‹ *Opposite.* The red-throated loon (*far left*), Red-throated loon distribution map (*upper right*), Red-throated loon nesting habitat in Norway's Svalbard archipelago at 77° north (*lower right*).

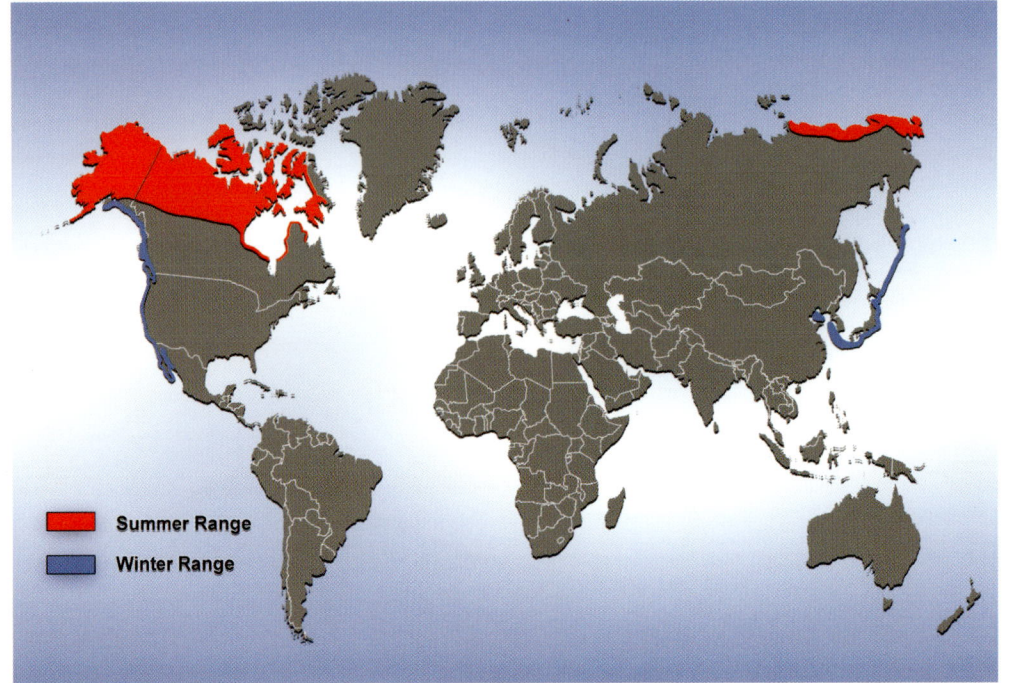

Summer Range

Winter Range

PACIFIC LOON (NORTH AMERICA) /
PACIFIC DIVER (EUROPE)
(French: Huart pacifique)

Scientific Name: *Gavia pacifica*. The epithet *pacifica* refers to the Pacific Ocean, the species' primarily wintering grounds. *See description of red-throated loon, above, for an explanation of the generic name Gavia.*

Field Identification: This handsome loon has a slim black bill, pale grey head and neck with bold black-and-white vertical stripes on the sides of its neck, and a dark throat, which appears black from a distance but may include purple or blue iridescence at close range. It has a conspicuous white chest and a black body with bold white spots on its back.

Formerly, two very similar subspecies were recognized: one breeding in North America and another in Eurasia. In 1985, the American Ornithologists' Union (now known as the American Ornithological Society) elevated each subspecies to full species status, with the North American subspecies becoming the Pacific loon and the Eurasian subspecies becoming the Arctic loon.

Size: Weight is 1.4 to 2.5 kilograms (3–5.5 lb.); length, 66 centimetres (26 in.); wingspan, 110 to 130 centimetres (43–51 in.).

Range: Nests in Arctic and boreal Canada and Alaska, as well as in a small corner of northeastern Siberia. Winters primarily along the Pacific coast of North America, from southeast Alaska to the tip of Baja California and in the northern half of the Gulf of California. A large proportion of the population winters in Mexico, but there is little information about its distribution. A small proportion of the population winters along the Pacific coast of Asia as far south as China and the Yellow Sea.

Status: Global population is 930,000 to 1,600,000. Appears to be increasing and is designated as a species of Least Concern by the IUCN (International Union for Conservation of Nature).

‹ *Opposite.* The Pacific loon (*far left*), Pacific loon distribution map (*upper right*), Pacific loon nesting habitat in the Hudson Bay Lowlands in northern Manitoba (*lower right*).

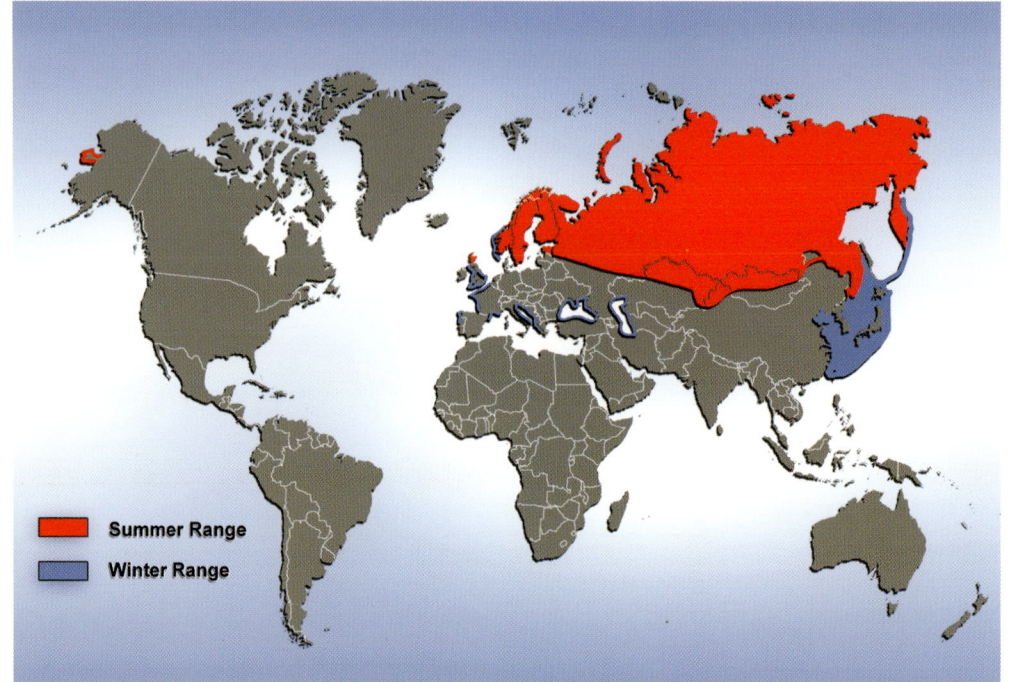

Summer Range

Winter Range

ARCTIC LOON (NORTH AMERICA) / BLACK-THROATED DIVER (EUROPE)
(French: Huart arctique)

Scientific Name: *Gavia arctica.* First described in 1758. The epithet *arctica* is Latin for northern or Arctic. *See description of red-throated loon, above, for an explanation of the generic name Gavia.*

Field Identification: Very similar in appearance to the Pacific loon and features a slim black bill, pale grey head and neck with bold black-and-white vertical stripes on the sides of its neck, and a dark throat, which appears black from a distance but may include purple or blue iridescence at close range. The nape of its neck is said to be darker than in the Pacific loon, with bolder vertical stripes on its neck, but frankly I find this hard to detect. Its most distinctive feature is a conspicuous white feather patch on its flanks, but this may not be visible if the bird is floating low in the water.

Size: Weight is 2.6 to 3.5 kilograms (5.7 to 7.7 lb.); length, 69 to 76 centimetres (27 to 30 in.); wingspan, 130 centimetres (51 in.).

Range: Nests across the northern forests of Eurasia, and winters in the offshore waters of northwestern Europe, in the Mediterranean and Black and Caspian Seas, as well as along the Pacific coasts of Asia, from the Kamchatka Peninsula in Russia to the southeastern coast of China. A small population of Arctic loons nests in the Seward Peninsula of western Alaska.

Status: Global population is 275,000 to 1.5 million. The overall trend is decreasing but it is still designated by the IUCN (International Union for Conservation of Nature) as being of Least Concern because of its large population size.

‹ *Opposite.* The Arctic loon (*far left*), Arctic loon distribution map (*upper right*), Arctic loon nesting habitat in southern Sweden (*lower right*)

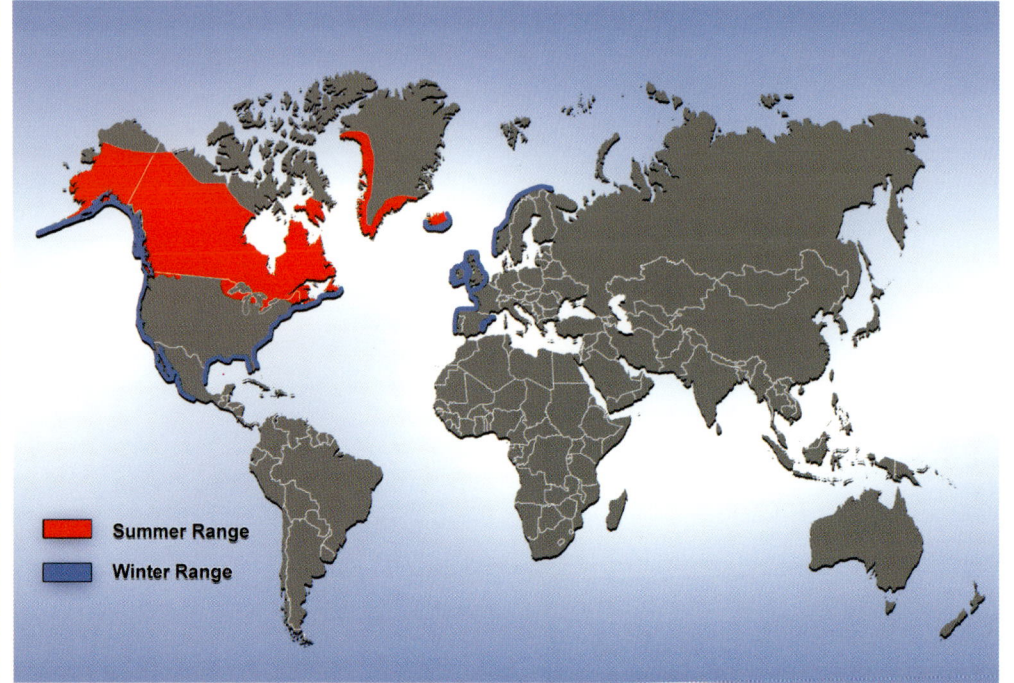

🟥	Summer Range
🟦	Winter Range

COMMON LOON (NORTH AMERICA) / GREAT NORTHERN DIVER (EUROPE)
(French: Huart à collier)

Scientific Name: *Gavia immer.* First described in 1764. The derivation of the specific epithet *immer* is unclear. It may have been derived from the Latin *immergo,* to immerse, or it could have arisen from the Swedish word for the blackened ashes of a fire, *emmer,* referring to the loon's black body plumage. *See description of red-throated loon, above, for an explanation of the generic name Gavia.*

Field Identification: From a distance, it simply looks like a large dark bird with a conspicuous white breast. At closer range, it has a large, sharp black beak; a black head, neck, and body; a white necklace; large rectangular white markings on its back; and white spotting on its sides and rump.

Size: Weight is 3.5 to 6 kilograms (7.8 to 13.2 lb.); body length, 81 centimetres (32 in.); wingspan, 140 to 160 centimetres (55 to 63 in.).

Range: Nests in a broad band of boreal and mixed forests across the breadth of North America, from Alaska to Newfoundland. It's also a common breeder in Iceland and in the treeless tundra areas flanking the coasts of southern Greenland. Winters inshore along both coasts in North America. On the Pacific side, it ranges from the Aleutian Islands in Alaska to the southern coast of Mexico, and on the Atlantic side, from Newfoundland to Florida and around the entire northern perimeter of the Gulf of Mexico. The birds in Greenland and Iceland are believed to winter in Iceland or along the Atlantic coast of Europe, from Finland to Portugal and into the western Mediterranean Sea.

Status: Global population is 612,000 to 640,000, of which 94 percent occur in Canada; roughly 25,000 are in the United States, and fewer than 3,000 are in Europe. Canada's population has declined over the last three decades, the combined consequence of acid rain, mercury pollution, climate warming, shoreline developments, and boating activity. Nonetheless, the IUCN (International Union for Conservation of Nature) lists the species as of Least Concern because of its wide range and large population size.

❮ *Opposite.* The common loon (*far left*), Common loon distribution map (*upper right*), Common loon nesting habitat in the northern boreal forests of Canada's Northwest Territories (*lower right*).

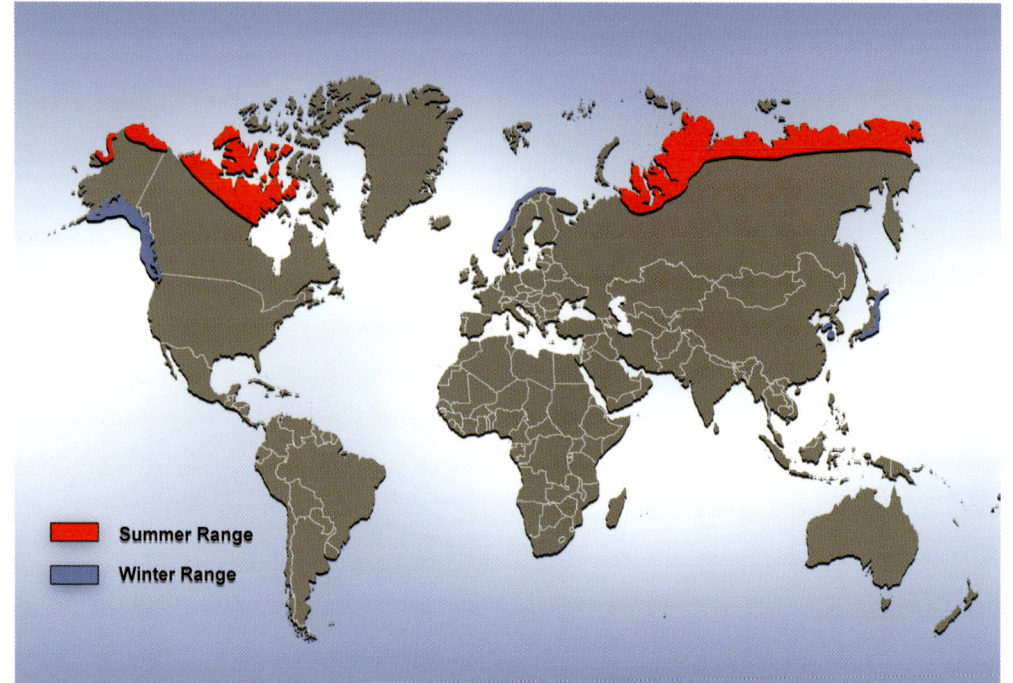

Summer Range
Winter Range

YELLOW-BILLED LOON (NORTH AMERICA) / WHITE-BILLED DIVER (EUROPE)
(French: Huart à bec jaune)

Scientific Name: *Gavia adamsii.* First described in 1859. The specific epithet adamsii honours Dr. Edward Adams, a British naval surgeon and naturalist who collected one of the first recorded specimens of yellow-billed loons while on several trips to Arctic Alaska in the 1800s. Adams, however, may not have been the first European to observe the species. Author Michael Dregni claims it was Dr. John Richardson, who accompanied Sir John Franklin on his polar voyage in 1825 to 1827. Richardson saw the loon at the mouth of the Coppermine River and thought at the time it was a new species not yet described. He was familiar with the common loon and noted the different bill colour. *See description of red-throated loon, above, for an explanation of the generic name Gavia.*

Field Identification: Almost identical to the common loon; from a distance simply looks like a large dark bird with a conspicuous white breast. At closer range, it has a black head, neck, and body; a white necklace; large rectangular white markings on its back; and white spotting on its sides and rump. It differs from the common loon in having a large, pale-yellow beak instead of a black one. Authorities also claim it has fewer white bars in its necklace and fewer and larger white rectangles on its back.

Size: Weight is 4 to 6.4 kilograms (8.8 to 14 lb.); length, 86 centimetres (34 in.); wingspan, 140 to 160 centimetres (55 to 63 in.).

Range: Nests in the tundra areas of Arctic Russia, Alaska, and Canada, and winters mainly off the coast of Norway, the eastern coasts of Japan, and the western coast of North America, typically north of 50°.

Status: Global population is 16,000 to 32,000. Designated by the IUCN (International Union for Conservation of Nature) as Near Threatened and is suspected of undergoing a moderately rapid population decline owing to unsustainable subsistence harvests.

‹ *Opposite.* The yellow-billed loon (*far left*), Yellow-billed loon distribution map (*upper right*), Yellow-billed loon nesting habitat on Victoria Island in western Nunavut, Canada (*lower right*).

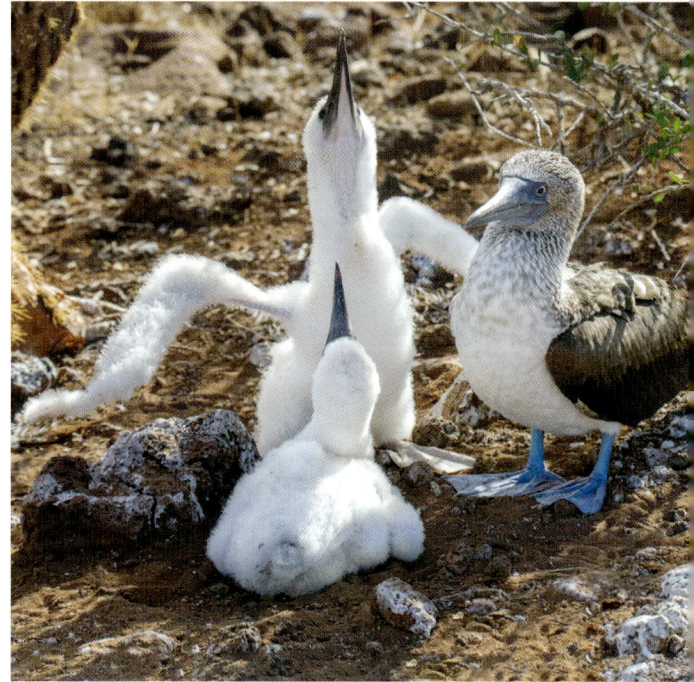

CHAPTER 4

Gone Fishin'

It was late April in the spruce and pine forests of northern Saskatchewan. The trees were draped with fresh snow that had fallen overnight, and the lakes were still largely capped with ice. For several days, my wife, Aubrey, and I had been monitoring the outlet of a large lake where the exiting current had melted a patch of open water large enough for common loons to land and take off. Two days earlier there had been five loons, nine the previous day, and that day there were sixteen. All were temporarily delayed, waiting for their nesting lakes to thaw. As we watched, one of the lingering loons caught a large, twenty-five-centimetre (10 in.) pike, and for next twenty minutes, the hapless fish was the stimulus for multiple boisterous chases, several ownership changes, and an attempted aerial piracy. Shortly after the loon caught the fish, it surrendered its catch to another loon that I assumed was its mate. The two birds swapped the fish back and forth several times. On numerous occasions, whichever loon had the fish securely wedged in its beak would make a brief dive lasting ten to fifteen seconds. I joked to Aubrey that maybe the loons were trying to drown the fish first before they swallowed it. Other loons floating nearby repeatedly chased the pike-possessing pair, presumably trying to pilfer their prize, but the wing-splashing pursuits always ended rather quickly. At one point, the lucky loon with the fish released its meal and let it float lifelessly on the water's surface. A bald eagle, perched at the top of a nearby white spruce, saw the floating fish and immediately swooped down, trying to snatch it away. At the last moment, the loon noticed the incoming eagle and reflexively grabbed the fish; with an alarmed yelp and a forceful splash, it successfully escaped underwater with the contested meal. In the end, one of the loons finally managed to get the fish's head fully inside its mouth, and after a dozen convulsive jerks swallowed the precious pike, ending the morning's drama.

THE SEABIRD SYNDROME

Most biologists informally define a seabird as one that makes its life from the sea, conceding that all of them must temporarily return to land to nest and raise a family. Most young loons spend at least the first two to three years of their lives permanently at sea while they mature. Each year after that, they spend five to six months during the winter living entirely on the ocean. Some loons, including the majority of red-throats and many

<
Opposite. Of the more than 10,000 species of birds worldwide, fewer than 300, or a mere 3 percent, are seabirds. Even though they are relatively few in number, seabirds display an impressive global diversity. Among them are (*clockwise from upper left*) Adélie penguins from Antarctica, black-browed albatrosses from the southern Atlantic Ocean, great frigatebirds from the legendary Galápagos Islands, blue-footed boobies from Mexico's Sea of Cortez, red-tailed tropicbirds from tropical Midway Island, and thick-billed murres from Arctic Norway.

> *Opposite.* An adult loon feeds a leech to an eight-week-old chick. Loons completely digest leeches in less than an hour, and thus the leeches may not be detected when the feces and stomach contents of loons are examined in dietary studies.

Pacific and yellow-billed loons, continue to forage at sea even while they are nesting on freshwater lakes. Veteran seabird ecologist Anthony Gaston, in his authoritative book *Seabirds: A Natural History*, unequivocally includes the loon family among the world's 300 or so species of seabirds. Gaston believes that most seabirds share a unique set of behavioural and ecological attributes, which he dubs "the seabird syndrome." He admits that some seabirds, such as the loons, may temporarily occupy freshwater habitats but nonetheless qualify for inclusion as seabirds because so much of their lives revolve around the ocean. The elements of the seabird syndrome include foraging at sea during the majority of the year, returning to land to breed, and the need for both parents to incubate and provision their young. Furthermore, the shared parenting by both adults leads to a limited difference in size and appearance between the sexes. A small clutch size of one or two eggs, typical of most seabirds, necessarily yields a low annual reproductive output, which predisposes to a long lifespan, which in turn permits reproduction to be deferred for several years. This constellation of attributes promotes multiyear pair bonds, which in turn places a premium on selecting the right partner. Consider

how the common loon demonstrates all of these traits. It has a potential lifespan of twenty-five to thirty years, may not begin to breed until it is six or seven years old, commonly forms pair bonds that last five or six years (but sometimes as long as twenty-three years), lays a clutch of just one or two eggs, and on average in Canada produces just 0.55 fledged chicks per pair per year. Few biologists doubt that loons are legitimate members of this specialized guild of birds.

BREAKFAST, LUNCH, AND DINNER

Loons are exclusively Northern Hemisphere birds. They range from the eighty-third parallel, where red-throated loons nest at the northern tip of Greenland—a mere 750 kilometres (466 mi.) from the North Pole—to the subtropical marine waters surrounding Taiwan on the twenty-second parallel, where some Arctic and red-throated loons usually overwinter. Despite this vast latitudinal range, spanning more than 6,500 kilometres (4,039 mi.) and embracing an enormous variety of freshwater and marine habitats, one type of prey dominates the diet of all five species of loon. That prey is fish. No matter where a loon lives, whether on fresh water or salt water, at least 80 percent

for loons to grab. A researcher in Ontario's Algonquin Park examined a dead loon and found twenty-five tags from hatchery trout in the bird's stomach. He couldn't determine if the loon had also preyed on wild trout, but loons being loons, it's likely the bird would target the most vulnerable fish it could find, and sluggish, naïve hatchery graduates would fit the bill.

On rare occasions, a loon tackles a meal too mighty to manage. In 1926, in a Pennsylvania lake, a dead loon washed ashore with a thirty-eight-centimetre (15 in.) pike perch (family Percidae) firmly wedged in its gaping mouth—the bird having choked to death on its victim. The man who found the loon took it to a taxidermist who said the sharp fins of the fish had deeply penetrated the bird's throat, making the prickly prey almost impossible to remove. The fish weighed over 800 grams (28 oz.). Renowned bird biologist Wayne Campbell recalls two incidents in coastal British Columbia in which dead common loons washed ashore with Pacific staghorn sculpins lodged in their throats. The sculpin is a common shallow-water species that grows up to twenty-three centimetres (9 in.) in length and has unusual antler-like spines projecting from its gill covers that it can raise as a defence mechanism.

The amount of time that a loon spends fishing each day depends on many factors. First, being a visual hunter, it needs daylight to illuminate the water, so no fishing happens at night. Tannin-stained or silt-laden waters can impair visibility and hamper a loon's hunting efforts. On the ocean, the state of the tidal cycle can be a further influence, with loons preferring to hunt when the tide is dropping, which may concentrate the fish in shallower water. Social circumstances can also impact a loon's foraging time. In the Yukon-Kuskokwim delta of Alaska, male Pacific loons foraged for 40 percent of their day during the prenesting period, just 3.3 percent during early incubation, and a mere 0.4 percent with newly hatched chicks. Once the chicks were larger, the male's daily foraging time jumped back up to 20 percent. Female Pacific loons were not influenced by the stage of the nesting cycle and consistently foraged 45 to 58 percent of the day throughout incubation and chick rearing. The males' foraging patterns were likely impacted by them patrolling and defending their territories, and evicting intruders intent on hostile takeover. This interesting topic will be covered in detail in Chapter 5. Aside from the variations during the nesting cycle, which occur in all of the species studied so far, most

loons, whether on their freshwater nesting lakes or wintering at sea, spend an average of 50 percent of their day foraging and the rest of the time loafing, resting, preening, and sparingly interacting and moving about.

The daily energy needs for any species of loon have not been studied in detail, but cormorants and fish-eating mergansers typically consume 15 to 25 percent of their body weight in prey each day. Assuming this percentage also applies to loons, researcher Digger Jackson estimated that a pair of Arctic loons nesting on a bonny loch in the Scottish Highlands would consume 300 to 500 kilograms (661 to 1,102 lb.) of fish during the breeding season, from March to September. In Jackson's study area, the loons were primarily eating small brown trout that weighed 30 to 150 grams (1 to 5 oz.) each. With prey that size, he calculated the total for the season would amount to several thousand fish. Jack Barr, working in Ontario's Algonquin Park in the 1970s, calculated that a breeding pair of common loons with two chicks would consume roughly 1,050 kilograms (2,315 lb.) of fish during a fifteen-week nesting period. With this kind of data, it's easy to understand why some human anglers might be hostile towards loons.

GO UNDER OR GO HUNGRY

Many seabirds scavenge. Great cormorants feed on dead harbour seals in coastal Spain, giant petrels gorge on rotting elephant seals and penguins in Antarctica, northern fulmars swarm over whale carcasses in the Arctic, and multiple species of gulls dine on the dead. I only know of one reported instance of loons feeding on carrion. One spring, in the Yukon-Kuskokwim delta, biologist Margaret Petersen watched Pacific loons eat large numbers of nine-spined sticklebacks. The fish had been frozen in icy ponds, and the loons scavenged the dead fish once the ice melted.

Though loons are proficient divers, they can sometimes feed themselves without diving at all. In Nunavut, I've watched red-throated loons snorkel in shallow water among the flooded stems of shoreline willows searching for fingerling Arctic char hiding in the shadows. At Storkersen Point, Alaska, researcher Robert Bergman reported that Pacific loons sometimes fed on caddisfly larvae (Trichoptera), tadpole shrimp (Notostraca), fairy shrimp (Anostraca), and water fleas (Cladocera) in shallow water along the shores of their nesting lakes. The loons would only submerge their head and neck, and occasionally

< *Opposite.* Early in the nesting season, the ownership of a territory may be challenged several times in one day, as was happening with this common loon ousting an intruder.

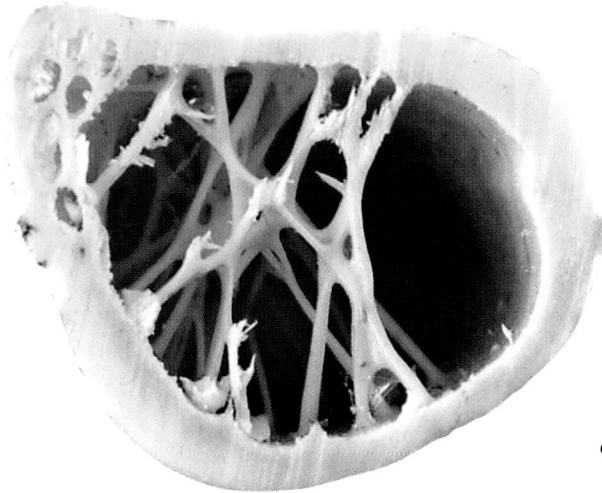

^ *Above.* These two cross sections of an avian humerus show the difference in bone structure between a heavy flying bird like the whooper swan (*top*), which has extensive skeletal air spaces, versus the very dense bones of a heavy diving bird such as the emperor penguin (*bottom*).

disturb the bottom sediments by "ploughing" with their bill to potentially expose the hidden invertebrates. In Scotland, early in the nesting season, Arctic loons may prey on spawning common frogs as they float near the surface in the shallow water along the shores of some of the lakes.

In spite of the fact that loons can sometimes find food without submerging, and in rare instances feed on carrion, their survival ultimately depends on diving and hunting underwater. For them, it's go under or go hungry. As previously described, loons are foot-propelled divers that rely on a suite of visual adaptations to capture their aquatic prey. But over the millennia, evolution endowed loons with even more assets and abilities than their enhanced underwater vision and large webbed feet.

A bird's skeleton can be an asset or a liability. A thin-boned skeleton filled with air spaces can dramatically reduce a bird's body weight and lessen the energy needed for flight. On the other hand, a skeleton with thickened bones and few air spaces can make a swimming bird less buoyant and better able to dive. The respiratory system in all birds consists of a small pair of lungs connected to multiple large air sacs scattered throughout the body cavity. In many birds, the air sacs even penetrate the large bones, such as the pelvis, sternum, the humerus of the wing, and the femur of the leg. Having air-filled bones, or *skeletal pneumaticity*, is one of the distinguishing features of birds, although the degree of pneumaticity varies among the world's over 10,000 species of birds. Researcher Nathan Smith looked at forty-two different waterbirds and compared their skeletal pneumaticity with their foraging ecology, and he gave each of them a score. Not surprisingly, frigatebirds had one of the highest pneumaticity scores, with a value of twenty-eight. The lightweight, air-filled skeleton of a frigatebird weighs less than its feathers do. Recall that these remarkable tropical seabirds may sometimes fly continuously for two months or more, sleeping on the wing. The red-billed tropicbird had a score of fifteen, and the black-footed albatross, twelve. Loons, and their close relatives the penguins, had virtually no air spaces in their bones, and Smith gave both of them a pneumaticity score of zero. He concluded that the nonpneumatized skeletons of divers, such as loons and penguins, were clearly adapted to minimize buoyancy and facilitate diving.

With no air spaces in their bones, loons delicately adjust their buoyancy by compressing their feathers and expelling air from their internal air sacs so that they gradually sink until sometimes only their eyes are showing. In this way, they can survey an area without being noticed and escape detection by rival loons if they happen to be trespassing on another's territory.

When a loon is actively foraging, it may precede a dive with peering to search underwater for potential prey. When it peers, it simply lowers its head into the water above the level of its eyes. Moments before a dive, the loon visibly compresses the feathers on its head, neck, and body, and then it sinks slightly but noticeably before it arches forward and disappears with a minimum of ripples. In 1919, avian chronicler Arthur Cleveland Bent colourfully described a diving loon: "The subaqueous rush of this formidable monster must cause consternation among the finny tribe."

Until relatively recently, the depth of loon dives was typically extrapolated from the measurement of the water depth in their foraging areas, and the time they spent underwater was determined by a person with a stopwatch. Loons, in general, make quite shallow dives, commonly in water less than thirty metres (98 ft.) deep, and often half that depth. As you might predict, the largest loons dive the deepest. In the Great Lakes, maximum depth records of seventy metres (230 ft.) have been reported for common loons that became accidentally tangled in gill nets and drowned. In 2018, the personal observations by researchers armed with a spotting scope and a stopwatch were finally replaced by high-tech wizardry. Using geotagged loons, biologist Kevin Kenow reported on the diving behaviour of common loons that were feeding in Lake Michigan during their autumn migration. He discovered that the birds were diving deeper than had been generally reported for loons observed on their nesting lakes. The Lake Michigan birds were making fast descents to maximum depths of forty-three to sixty metres (141 to 197 ft.), depending on where they were in the lake. The deep-diving loons stayed at depth throughout most of their dives and finished off with a rapid ascent to the surface. Such dive profiles are generally characteristic of birds foraging on an ocean or lake bottom.

One could predict that the red-throated loon, being the smallest of the loons, would make shallower dives than its larger relative the common loon. In 2019, biologist James Duckworth attached a time-depth recorder (a digital gizmo used successfully for many years in penguins) to a red-throated loon in Finland and recorded its diving behaviour for fourteen days between early June and early August. Throughout the observational period, the red-throat foraged in freshwater habitats and not in the ocean as they often do. The Finnish loon routinely foraged in water just five metres (16 ft.) deep—a dramatic difference when compared with the common loons in Lake Michigan. Personally, I have watched wintering red-throats hunt along the coastline of British Columbia close to a sandy beach where the water was barely a metre (3 ft.) deep. Although Duckworth's study focused on a single bird, it supported the belief that the smallest of the loons would necessarily forage in shallower water than the larger species.

Most loons make dives that last less than a minute. In multiple studies of common loons, dives averaged thirty-three to sixty-two seconds. But, once again, Kenow's study of migrating common loons in Lake Michigan upset the applecart.

In his study, birds often plunged to depths of forty metres and were underwater for an average of 139 seconds, and a quarter of all dives lasted 120 seconds or more. The longest dive reported by Kenow was 230 seconds. Compare this to the dive times of red-throated loons off the coast of British Columbia, which averaged thirty seconds when foraging inshore and forty-one seconds when offshore. In a Polish study by Polak and Ciach, Arctic loons wintering on inland lakes made short dives lasting just twelve to seventeen seconds. Researchers attributed the brevity of the dives to the shallowness of the water. In a study in California's Monterey Bay, Pacific loons made dives averaging seventy-seven seconds, intermediate between the larger common loons in the area whose dives averaged ninety-four seconds and the smaller red-throated loons that were underwater for an average of forty-nine seconds.

The duration of a loon's dive is influenced by the type of prey it's hunting, the abundance of prey, water clarity and depth, search time, pursuit time, and the time of day, which affects the depth of light penetration. Sharp-eyed researchers calculating the duration times of dives can sometimes be fooled by "sneaky" loons that surface, breathe, and discreetly dive again, leaving barely a ripple on the surface. Loons can also cover great distances underwater, sometimes as much as several hundred metres, making it difficult to track them. Such tricky diving behaviour has led in the past to false claims of dive durations lasting ten to fifteen minutes. Having said that, longtime loon researcher James Paruk claims he has recorded dive times of over four minutes in common loons wintering in Lake Jocassee in South Carolina. As they say in Missouri, "You've got to show me."

James Duckworth's detailed study of a red-throated loon in Finland provided further fascinating detail on the bird's foraging pattern. The monitored red-throat made an average of 425 dives per day, spread over seventeen foraging bouts. Some individual foraging bouts contained fewer than ten dives, but the longest one amounted to 339 dives and lasted for over three hours. The information logged in the time-depth recorders revealed that the loon moved to shallower water during twilight. In full daylight, its maximum dive depth was 6.2 metres (20 ft.) versus 4.4 metres (14 ft.) during twilight. Duckworth thought the difference was explained by the reduced penetration of sunlight during twilight.

Evolution, through the process of natural selection,

‹ *Opposite.* This common loon was peering underwater, hunting in a small patch of open water on a lake that was still largely covered with ice. It never brought any prey to the surface, so I never learned what it was eating.

❮ *Left.* When foraging, a red-throated loon may simply pop its head above the water, breathe, and dive again.

honed loons to be as skilled at diving as they need to be to successfully survive and procreate, but compared to other air-breathing divers, loons are amateurs. Among birds, penguins are the undisputed master divers. King penguins have been recorded diving to depths of 325 metres (1,066 ft.), and big-bodied emperors can plunge to 564 metres (1,850 ft.) and stay submerged for nearly twenty-eight minutes. The leatherback turtle, the largest living sea turtle, hunts jellyfish at depths of 1,230 metres (4,035 ft.), and southern elephant seals go even deeper to 2,388 metres (7,835 ft.) and stay submerged for more than an hour and a half. The deepest recorded air-breathing diver is the bull sperm whale, which stalks bottom-dwelling sharks 3,050 metres (10,006 ft.) down and remains underwater for almost two and half hours. Even some naked apes, *Homo sapiens*, can out dive a loon. In 2016, William Trubridge set a record for freediving without the aid of swim fins when he kicked his way down to 124 metres (406 ft.) and held his breath for four minutes and thirty-four seconds!

All air-breathing divers must carry oxygen with them to fuel their metabolism during the dive, storing it in their lungs, blood, and muscles. To make prolonged, deep dives, seals have

❯ Two of the deepest-diving vertebrates are the leatherback sea turtle (*top*) and the southern elephant seal (*bottom*). The leatherback turtle is the world's largest turtle, sometimes stretching over two metres (6.5 ft.) in length and weighing over 500 kilograms (1,102 lb.). The southern elephant seal, the largest seal in the world, is also a heavyweight, with large bulls tipping the scales at over 4,500 kilograms (9,920 lbs). Both can make dives to depths of 1,000 metres (3,280 ft.) or more.

a higher blood volume, more oxygen-binding hemoglobin in their red blood cells, and more oxygen-binding myoglobin in their muscles than land mammals of a similar size. Seals also respond to submergence with a diving reflex in which their heart rate slows and blood is preferentially redirected to vital organs, such as the brain and heart, to conserve oxygen. None of these diving adaptations has been reported to exist in loons. It may simply be that loons normally make such comparatively short, shallow dives that they never exceed the normal oxygen stores that are present in all birds, and thus they have no need for any specialized physiological adaptations.

To successfully capture prey underwater, a diving bird needs speed and manoeuvrability. In a recent fascinating study, biologist Glenna Clifton looked at the swimming expertise and turning abilities of diving common loons. It turns out that the loon is a bit of an underwater slowpoke. In straight swimming, it putters along at 0.16 to 0.86 metres per second (0.5 to 2.8 ft./sec) compared to 1.2 metres per second (3.9 ft./sec) for foot-propelled grebes and 1.6 metres per second (5.2 ft./sec) for web-footed cormorants. As evolution would have it, common loons also turn slowly compared to other divers, turning at a rate of

287° per second versus 576° per second in penguins and 690° per second in sea lions. Although loons are not particularly fast underwater and make relatively slow turns, they do excel when it comes to the tightness of their turns, which are twice as sharp as either sea lions or penguins. Clifton convincingly concluded, "Sea lions, penguins and cetaceans typically hunt in open water, requiring them to out-chase their prey. In contrast, loons primarily search for prey on the ocean or lake floor, often probing along rocks then quickly snatching any flushed animals.... This strategy relies on maneuvering in relatively tight spaces, but at slow speeds, until quickly accelerating to capture a fish at close range. Additionally, a potentially important difference between loons and all previously studied turning animals is their long and flexible neck." Clifton's study may explain why different species of perch are often a favourite target of many loons. The typical escape behaviour of perch is erratic zigzag swimming, which makes them susceptible to capture because of the loons' ability to turn sharply and strike while doing so.

Most of the time, an observer gazing through a spotting scope from shore has no idea if a foraging loon was successful or, if it was, what critter it caught. The reason? Loons swallow most of their prey underwater and can presumably catch more than one prey item in a successful dive before surfacing to breathe. It's only when the prey is intended for a chick, or is especially large and perhaps difficult to control and subdue, that a loon surfaces before swallowing it.

In North Carolina, researcher Gilbert Grant watched common loons surface with blue crabs, speckled crabs, and mole crabs, as well as six different kinds of fish, which he was able to identify while watching with a spotting scope and binoculars. Crabs usually took a little time for the loons to consume, as they needed to be crushed and dismembered first. In one case, a loon took more than two minutes to smash and thrash a crab that was just four centimetres (1.5 in.) long.

Loons have no hook on the end of their beak, so they have trouble tearing large prey into pieces. Gilbert found that captured flounders always gave the loons trouble. The birds had to repeatedly stab and tear the fish apart before they could swallow it. In Nantucket Bay, Massachusetts, a researcher examined a dead loon that had fifteen flounders in its stomach, each ten to fifteen centimetres (4 to 6 in.) wide. Apparently, the appetite of at least one loon wasn't dampened by the handling time.

‹ *Opposite.* The gape on a loon determines how large a fish it can swallow. Loons have a wide skull and strong muscles attached to their jaws and neck to help them consume bulky prey, such as this rainbow trout.

The mouth of every loon is a one-way trap. A loon's tongue and palate are covered with stiff, keratinized denticles that improve the bird's grip on wiggly, slippery prey, and the spines point backward to keep food moving in one direction—inside.

From the mouth and throat, the food passes down the esophagus to a large glandular stomach, called the *proventriculus*, where the meal is bathed in acid and digestive enzymes. The next stop is the muscular gizzard that crushes and grinds the meal. To help in the pulverizing process, loons have stones in their gizzard. In 2001, biologist Christian Franson and three colleagues published *Size Characteristics of Stones Ingested by Common Loons.* The paper was filled with the kind of delicious biological trivia that makes me salivate. The researchers found that 98 percent of common loons had stones in their stomach, typically ten to twenty small, pea-sized pebbles. The stones had an average length of 12.5 millimetres (0.5 in.), with the largest one found being roughly twice that size. The researchers were concerned that loons might inadvertently pick up discarded lead fishing sinkers from lake bottoms in their search for stones. Lead poisoning is one of the leading causes of loon mortality in the New England states, and the scientists were trying to mount a case to justify the banning of lead in fishing tackle. This important topic will be covered in more detail in Chapter 8.

Many fish-eating birds, such as herons, grebes, cormorants, gulls, terns, and kingfishers, periodically regurgitate pellets of indigestible bones, teeth, and scales. Not so in loons. The gizzard in a loon, assisted by the multiple stones it ingests, is such a powerful organ that it capably pulverizes fish bones, the heavy defensive spines of catfish, and the tough chitinous exoskeletons of crabs and other invertebrates with relative ease. Every part of a meal is digested, and the birds have no leftovers to regurgitate.

When loons are wintering on the ocean, swallowing

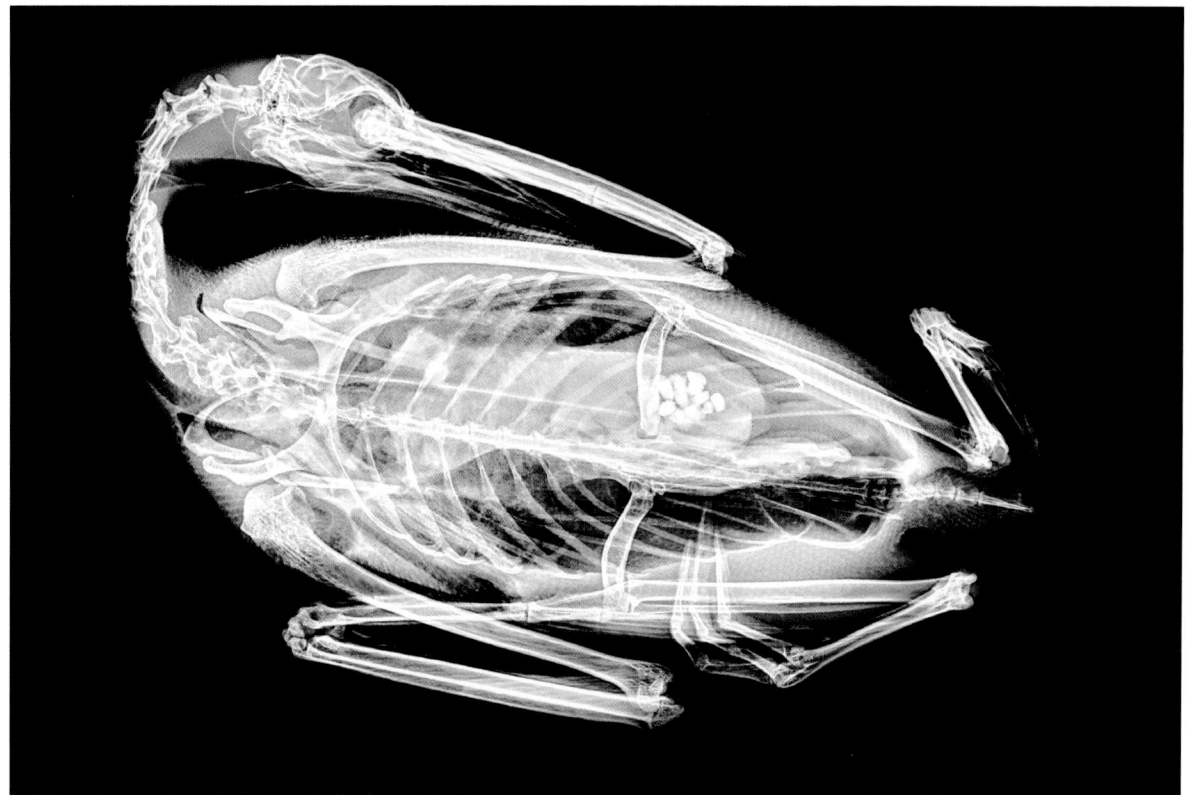

prey underwater is virtually impossible to do without also swallowing a fair amount of salty seawater. Since the kidneys of a loon are only slightly better at excreting this salt load than are our own, the loon, in common with all other seabirds, has two specialized salt glands to help rid itself of the extra salt it accidentally ingests. Each gland is about the size of an almond, and there is one above each eye, cradled in a depression on the outside of the bird's skull. These salt glands drain into a loon's nose, and when a bird first finishes a foraging bout, drops of salty water run off the tip of its beak.

Some of what goes in the front end of a loon eventually passes out the rear end. Typically, when loons, and most other seabirds, need to defecate, they simply lift their tail feathers wherever they are and let the feces fly. I have spent a lot of time in penguin nesting colonies and the evacuation process in these crowded gatherings can be especially messy. In the Falkland Islands, I watched the reaction of a southern rockhopper penguin that was within range when its neighbour let the guano go. The rockhopper took a full blast in the face. The plastered penguin simply shook its head, snorted, and allowed the wet goo to slowly drip from its beak and golden

crest. I've never seen any species of loon defecate while it was flying or quietly sitting on its nest. If an incubating loon is suddenly frightened, however, it may defecate on its eggs as it hurriedly escapes. Most often, all an observer sees when a loon defecates is a sudden spray of white in the water that quickly dissipates. In western Alberta in August 2020, I watched an eight-week-old common loon chick climb ashore, spin around to face the water, defecate, and immediately slip back into the lake. Three days later, I saw the young loon do the same thing in the same location, so I paddled over for a closer look. The grass along the shoreline was flattened and there were many streaks of old and recent whitewash. Clearly, the spot had been

^ *Above.* In this X-ray of a common loon that died of unknown causes, more than a dozen small stones are visible in its gizzard. All loons swallow stones to help them pulverize the bones and spines they ingest in their food.

Top Left and Bottom. The white strips on the grassy shorelines show the defecation site of a family of common loons in western Alberta, and that of yellow-billed loons in Arctic Canada.

used many times. A year later, when I was observing loons in Arctic Canada, I watched a Pacific loon, as well as a yellow-billed loon, also climb on shore to defecate. In the case of the yellow-bill, I found a seven-metre (23 ft.) section of shoreline where the moss was matted down and splattered with at least twenty streaks of whitewash. Other evidence may have been washed away by the rain two days earlier. In the 1980s, pioneer loon researcher Judith McIntyre suggested that this kind of ritualized defecation might be a territorial marker visible to loons flying overhead. Harry Vogel, a senior biologist with the Loon Preservation Committee, wrote to me in an email, "I would not describe this as a common behavior, but it has been reported in the past, and some loons will do it habitually—not sure if all the time, but at least occasionally. I have heard it described as a territorial marking behavior but since it has been reported in chicks and adults that doesn't seem likely to me. It may be just a habitual 'don't foul the water where you swim' behavior of some loons." The purpose of this unusual behaviour is one more tantalizing mystery in the lives of these fascinating birds.

FUSSING WITH FEATHERS

After a bout of diving and dining, the focus of every loon usually turns to preening. Judith McIntyre, in her seminal book *The Common Loon: Spirit of Northern Lakes*, described it well: "Care of the feathers occupies loons throughout the day. After diving, sitting on the nest, or engaging in social interactions, they preen, bathe, shake, and rearrange their feathers. Preening realigns the individual barbs lining both sides of the feather shaft. These tend to come unhooked during physical activity, and if feathers are to provide a protective covering, all the parts must stay 'zipped' together to form a smooth and waterproof surface."

Typically, a preening session lasts five to fifteen minutes, but it can sometimes continue much longer. One protracted fight I watched, in which the combatants exchanged vicious stabbing blows and an exhausting three-minute, wing-rowing water chase, ended when the intruder narrowly escaped among some shoreline vegetation. He hid there for about fifteen minutes waiting for the victorious territory owner to swim away. When the defeated loon eventually emerged, he spent over thirty minutes preening his dishevelled, bloodied plumage before finally flying away. He was lucky to be alive.

A loon usually begins a preening session by dipping its bill in water or squeezing oil from its uropygial gland at the base of its tail, which it then spreads on the feathers of its back and shoulders. One of the next steps is a careful *head rub*, in which the fastidious bird vigorously throws its head backward and rubs it against the previously anointed feathers, transferring oil onto its head and neck. One of the loon's most noticeable feather-tending behaviours is the so-called *rolling preen*, in which the bird rolls on its side, conspicuously exposing the white plumage of its belly. While in this position, it uses its bill to methodically comb through the feathers of its underside, straightening and oiling them thoroughly. Some claim that the glistening whiteness of a loon's belly is visible more than a kilometre (0.6 mi.) away.

For decades, every book of ornithology claimed it was the oil from the uropygial gland that made a bird's feathers waterproof. As I like to say, "Science will set you free." In a 2011 paper, Arie Rijke and William Jesser examined water penetration and repellency in feathers. Waterbirds, such as loons, produce copious amounts of oil and spend much time preening, but, and this is a big *but*, analysis of the chemical and

❯ *Right.* A bathing Pacific loon may intersperse vigorous splashing with wing flapping, belly preening, and rollovers onto its back. Loons preen much more frequently than they bathe, which is more common after mating or a bout of incubation.

physical properties of the oil failed to show that it was directly responsible for the water repellency of a feather. When feathers were experimentally stripped of all their oil, they continued to repel water. It was the interlocking structure of the feather barbs that made them waterproof, not the oil. It seems that the oil serves primarily as a lubricant to keep feathers sliding smoothly and from becoming brittle.

Sometimes a preening session will start calmly and then suddenly escalate into a full-blown bout of bathing. One time, when I was shadowing a pair of common loons from a distance in a canoe, one of the birds, which had just started to preen, suddenly began splashing wildly. To my surprise, it abruptly flipped upside down, exposing its entire white underside, and continued to vigorously beat its wings even though its head and neck were completely underwater. It did this comical manoeuvre six or seven times. It finished off the bathing session with a calm preening sequence and an energetic wing flap.

CHAPTER 5
Summertime's Critical Window

It was June 23 in the first summer of the new millennium. Aubrey and I had been camped for a week in a remote area of Victoria Island, Nunavut, surrounded by picturesque rolling tundra studded with innumerable crystalline lakes, herds of shaggy muskoxen, and an enchanting mix of nesting Arctic birds. Among the avian delights were a dozen varieties of crooning sandpipers and plovers, resplendent king eiders, long-legged sandhill cranes, sabre-winged Sabine's gulls, rough-legged hawks, and three species of exquisite northern loons. On that memorable day, we were perched on a hill near our camp watching an ermine deliver collared lemmings to its hungry young sequestered in a rocky crevice. In a quiet moment, when I scanned the surroundings for *oomingmak*, the bearded beasts known as muskoxen, I spotted a red-throated loon building a nest on the top of a tiny submerged mound three metres (9.8 ft.) out from the edge of a shallow lake. A day later, I set up a photo blind to observe the breeding pair more closely. The lip of the nest was barely a centimetre (0.5 in.) above the water surface, and I worried that waves might swamp it during the windstorms that commonly swept through the area. The next afternoon, when both loons were gone from the lake, I stripped down to my underwear and went wading in the icy water. I tore off several large clumps of wet sod from the shoreline and added them to the top of the nest to elevate its surface, which cradled a single olive-coloured egg. The following day, the nest had a second egg in it, and the birds had contentedly settled into their renovated home. A week later, after a stormy night with winds gusting to fifty kilometres per hour (30 mph), I anxiously checked on the loons and was initially pleased to see one of the pair perched on the nest. As I walked to my blind, the loon slipped into the water, something the unwary bird had never done before, and I saw that both its eggs were missing. I waded out and found the eggs resting on the bottom of the lake. The embryos would be dead, so there was no point in retrieving the lost clutch. Doing so might fool the loon pair into pointlessly incubating eggs that would never hatch. The next day, on July 4, the pair abandoned the lake to the wind and the wilderness.

WINGING NORTH

The spring migratory movements of loons have been studied most in North America. Starting in March, along both coasts of the continent, an undeniable restlessness stirs within every

< *Opposite.* I added sod to this red-throated loon nest to elevate it above the water surface, hoping to prevent it from flooding. Despite that, the large waves produced during a strong windstorm flushed the eggs out of the nest a week after the birds started to incubate.

^ *Above.* Loons are daytime migrants, landing at the end of each day to rest and forage.

territorial fervour of drumming ruffed grouse, triggering the familiar hooting of courting barred owls, and swelling every tree bud in the forest with the prospect of renewal.

Loons migrate during the day and make their way north in stages, following one of three migration routes: a Pacific coastal route, an Atlantic coastal route, or an inland route from the Gulf of Mexico through the centre of the continent, stopping on large reservoirs and the Great Lakes as they filter north. As previously discussed, loons are heavy-bodied birds with relatively small wings, and because of weight constraints, they can't afford to significantly pad their bodies in advance of migration with heavy layers of fat to sustain them on lengthy flights. As a result, migrating loons land at the end of each day and often stay in one location for several days while they forage and prepare for the next stage of their travels. Some that have wintered in the Gulf of Mexico, or off the coast of California or Florida, may take a month or two to reach their summer destinations, while others, such as the common loons in New England, may fly a mere three to four hours, moving inland from the ocean areas where they wintered to the lakes where they will breed. During spring migration, groups of 200 to 1,000

adult loon. The increasing hours of daylight, known as the *photoperiod*, cues their behaviour through a chain of hormones and fuels in them an impatient urge to migrate from the familiar ocean waters of their wintering grounds to the northern freshwater lakes where they will nest. The loons are not alone in their restlessness. On the Pacific coast, these same light-driven cues are prompting mother grey whales with newborn calves to migrate north to reap the summertime flush of invertebrates in the Bering and Chukchi Seas. It also prompts harlequin ducks, in their breeding finery, to leave the ocean and fly to food-rich mountain streams in the Sierras and Rocky Mountains. In the East, on the Atlantic coast, the photoperiod is awakening the

Pacific loons may temporarily gather in California's Monterey Bay, and resting flocks of several thousand have been seen along the Oregon coast. In the East, thousands of red-throated loons may stop and gather in Lake Ontario in April and May. This leisurely stop-and-go migration pattern, so typical of many loons, is in stark contrast to the habits of many shorebird migrants. The bar-tailed godwit, for example, doubles its body weight in a frenzy of feeding and then migrates between Alaska and New Zealand in an eight- or nine-day nonstop flight of roughly 11,500 kilometres (7,146 mi.)—the direct consequence of a wing loading that evolved for lengthy flight versus one designed for a heavy-bodied, diving seabird such as the loon.

No species of loon is known to fly in formation, despite the proven benefits. By flying in their well-known V formation, migrating Canada geese enjoy roughly a 10 percent energy savings, which translates into a greater flight range and greater possible reserves at the end of a flight—energy savings that would seem desirable to a migrating loon. Nonetheless, migrating loons typically fly alone or in pairs, trios, or foursomes; they also fly in small, loose groups, up to a dozen or two strong, with individuals often flying several hundred metres (218 yd.), or even up to a kilometre (0.6 mi.), apart. Since loons don't winter with their mates, the members of such groups have no special connection to each other.

When loons are on the move, daily numbers can be staggering. One spring, observers north of Santa Barbara, California, counted 3,891 common loons, 4,355 red-throated loons, and 22,768 Pacific loons flying north in one sixty-eight-hour period. All the birds were presumed to have wintered in coastal Mexican waters. Elsewhere, researchers at Whitefish Point Bird Observatory in Michigan's Upper Peninsula routinely see over 1,000 common loons passing overhead in a day, with as many as 700 in a single hour.

⌃ *Above.* A common loon in migration is generally not influenced by the temperature, cloud cover, or the speed and direction of the wind. The loon will even fly into strong headwinds. Only heavy rain and fog will force it to land. In northern Wisconsin in late May 2021, several dozen common loons were forced to land during a spring storm. One of the grounded birds was seen with a veil of ice on its wings.

When migrating over water, loons are often visible from shore, flying low and fast over the surface. Red-throated loons, for example, commonly fly between five and seventy metres (16 to 230 ft.) above the water at speeds between fifty and seventy kilometres per hour (31 to 43 mph). Sometimes, they fly just beyond the breaking waves. The larger loon species tend to fly somewhat farther from shore, often within a few kilometres of the coastline, but at times they fly as far as thirty to forty kilometres (18 to 25 mi.) offshore, where researchers can track them with sensitive radar.

Over land, migrating loons fly much higher than they do over water, and they often cannot be seen without binoculars. For example, common loons routinely fly over land at altitudes of 1,500 to 2,700 metres (4,921 to 8,858 ft.), where there is less turbulence from thermals. In theory, airspeed increases by 5 percent for every kilometre (0.6 mi.) above sea level, so a loon flying at two kilometres (1.2 mi.) can theoretically increase its airspeed by 10 percent. Such high-flying common loons can zip along at 113 to 138 kilometres per hour (70–85 mph), and even faster if they have a tailwind. Temperatures are also cooler at higher altitudes, which benefits exercising big-bodied birds, such as loons, which are prone to overheating.

In 2014, dogged loon researcher James Paruk reported on two wintering loons, a male and a female. He fitted each with a satellite transmitter off the coast of Louisiana and followed as they migrated north to Saskatchewan. The details paint two surprisingly different migration pictures, despite the same coastal start location.

The male loon left Adams Bay, Louisiana, on April 11 on a more or less direct route to Canada, stopping at the end of the first day on Pine Lake in Tennessee, having flown 725 kilometres (450 mi.). From there, he made eight more stops, with daily distances varying between 22 and 909 kilometres (13.6 and 565 mi.). Six of the stopovers lasted just a day or two, but he loitered in a reservoir in Tennessee for nine days and in Lake Michigan for fifteen days before gradually flying on to northern Saskatchewan in the ten days after that. In total, the male took thirty-six days to cover 3,840 kilometres (2,386 mi.).

The female loon left coastal Louisiana five days later, on April 16, and instead of heading inland on a northward routing as the male had done, she flew east to coastal Alabama and then northeast 1,126 kilometres (700 mi.) on a nonstop flight to a reservoir in North Carolina. The following morning, she flew another 331 kilometres

> *Opposite.* Boreal forests cover more than half of the large Canadian province of Saskatchewan, where there are an estimated 2,000 breeding pairs of common loons.

(206 mi.) to reach the Patuxent River in Maryland, where she stayed for the next ten days. After foraging and resting in Maryland, the loon spent the next three weeks flying on to Saskatchewan, making seven short stops plus one long stop of eleven days in Manitoba. In total, the female also took thirty-six days to complete her migration but covered a distance of 4,538 kilometres (2,820 mi.), 698 kilometres (434 mi.) more than the male.

LOCATION, LOCATION, LOCATION

In springtime, many loons return north only to find their nesting lakes still frozen over, forcing them to wait for the ice to melt. Alan Hutchinson described the situation in his book *Just Loons: A Wildlife Watcher's Guide:* "These returning birds scout and probe ahead, testing to see if the ice has gone. They can cover hundreds of miles a day in these pursuits. When not on flying searches, they spend the day on large bodies of water, coastal bays or lakes that have thawed, feeding and waiting in anticipation of spring's arrival farther north." Great numbers of loons can gather in these ice-free staging areas, and disappear just as quickly. Take Centerville Lake in Minnesota, for example. In the spring of 1950, biologist Sigurd Olson monitored the lake and recorded the arrival and departure of local common loons. That year, the lake became ice-free on April 19. Within a day or two, 200 to 300 loons had settled on the lake. Roughly a week later, the number had dropped to just twenty-five, and by May 6, all the loons were gone. In the Arctic, persistent leads of open water along the edges of the sea ice and open river mouths are common staging areas for yellow-billed, Pacific, and red-throated loons. As Hutchinson indicated, it's probable that waiting loons make frequent reconnaissance flights, perhaps on a daily basis, checking on the status of frozen nesting lakes, and as soon as a nesting lake has enough open water to land safely, they will. I saw just how soon loons will occupy a melting lake on April 30, 2021. A lake I was

‹ *Above.* In early May, twenty-eight common loons gathered in a small patch of open water on a partly frozen lake in northern Saskatchewan while they waited for their breeding lakes to thaw. Four days later, all but six had left.

‹ *Opposite.* A loon will often preen after a lengthy flight. The bird's flexible neck enables it to reach most areas of its body.

monitoring in Alberta looked completely covered with ice, but when I checked again with my binoculars, I saw a pair of loons swimming in a narrow ribbon of open water, barely two metres (6.6 ft.) wide, along the eastern shore.

All nesting loons are territorial. In birds, a territory is an exclusive area defended for the purpose of mating, nesting, and rearing young. In loons, a territory may also include exclusive feeding areas, but not always. For example, when a loon of any species leaves its nesting lake to forage in the ocean, it does not try to defend a specific feeding area and exclude others from using it, although it may temporarily deter another loon from foraging too close to it.

Breeding is the only reason loons migrate from the ocean to freshwater lakes every year, and all of their decisions regarding a territory revolve around finding a plot of real estate where they can successfully rear young. As any real estate agent will attest, the value of a home is closely tied to location, location, location. A loon has an unconscious checklist of qualities it wants in a nesting territory. It needs a suitable shoreline where it can build a nest, a shoreline that is not too steep, high, or thickly vegetated, and one where the adjacent water is deep enough to allow for a rapid dive to safety if necessary. Other desirable features include a nest site that has good visibility to watch for predators and trespassing loons, and one that isn't exposed to dangerous waves during stormy weather or subject to scouring by wind-driven ice. In Arctic latitudes, the loon nesting season often begins when the central part of the breeding lakes is still capped with ice. During windstorms, the ice moves around and sometimes piles up along the shore, where it can block a loon from reaching its nest or completely scour a nest away. In addition, vulnerable chicks need a nursery area where the water is shallow, the predators few, and the food abundant. An island can fill all of these needs, and in lakes with them, islands are selected by prospecting loons more than any other nesting location.

All loon species occupy one of three types of territory. There is the *whole-lake territory*, in which outsiders are aggressively excluded from every corner of the lake. There is also the *partial-lake territory*, in which a nesting pair defends just a portion of a lake. This might mean two pairs of yellow-billed loons share a single lake on Banks Island, Nunavut, or that five pairs of Pacific loons partition a medium-size lake in the Hudson Bay Lowlands. It could also mean twenty pairs of common loons

subdivide a very large lake in the Canadian Shield country of northern Ontario. Some of the largest lakes attract even more breeding pairs. For example, Moosehead Lake in Maine, with an area of over 30,000 hectares (74,000 ac.), is home to roughly fifty breeding pairs of common loons. In the 1980s, researcher Keith Yonge estimated 200 adults had territories on Hanson Lake in northern Saskatchewan. Although Hanson Lake is only 4,123 hectares (10,188 ac.) in area, Yonge believed it was attractive to loons because of its 221 islands, its highly irregular shoreline with numerous pockets and bays, and its very light recreational and commercial usage.

Until recently, researchers didn't realize that loons sometimes defend a third type of territory, one with more than a single lake in it. These so-called *multi-lake territories* have been reported for every species of loon except yellow-bills. Multi-lake territories are most common in red-throated loons, which may simultaneously defend up to four different lakes, all within a few hundred metres to two kilometres (0.6 to 1.2 mi.) of each other. The red-throats always use one of the lakes for nesting and the others for escape, loafing, and preening. Since most nesting red-throats forage primarily in the ocean,

‹ *Opposite.* In spring, wind-driven ice on freshwater lakes can scour the shoreline and completely destroy a loon's nest.

the other lakes are not used for feeding, but such is not the case with the other loon species, which often use the additional lakes to meet the food needs of their family. Multi-lake use can produce false and inflated population estimates, so researchers always strive to identify the individual loons occupying the different lakes. They are especially attentive to this in areas with predominantly small lakes, where multi-lake territories are more common.

Every general research paper on loons talks about the size of the territories the different species defend. The typical story is that the biggest species, the common and yellow-billed loons, maintain the largest territories, often larger than fifty to sixty hectares (123 to 148 ac.). The smallest species, the red-throated loon, naturally uses the smallest lakes, sometimes ones just 0.05 hectares (0.12 ac.) in size. The mid-size Arctic and Pacific loons commonly defend territories whose sizes are between these two extremes. This neat and tidy size partitioning works some of the time but not all of the time. Yellow-billed loons have been reported nesting on lakes as small as 0.1 hectares (0.2 ac.), and red-throated loons on Bathurst Island in the Canadian High Arctic commonly nest on larger lakes than usual, averaging fifty-four hectares hectares (133 ac.) in size. The red-throats are able to do this primarily because no other loon species is present on Bathurst Island to challenge them.

The lake size that any loon species ultimately selects depends on a number of factors. Are there lakes of different sizes in the nesting area, or are they all large or all small? Are there other species of loons competing for the same lakes? Among the loon species there is a definite hierarchy based on body size; the bigger species generally dominate the smaller ones. Latitude also influences the lake size a loon will choose. In the High Arctic, where multiple loon species often share the same tundra areas, the nesting season is brief and limited to a narrow critical window. At these latitudes, the ice in small, shallow lakes disappears sooner than it does in larger, deeper lakes, so the birds can nest earlier and take advantage of this. But these same shallow lakes also freeze over sooner in autumn and may not give a loon family enough time to fledge their chicks. All of these variables influence the selection of a territory.

Common loons have been studied more than the other four species combined, and many of the exciting new discoveries in nesting ecology were made in common loons. Nonetheless, I

think it is fair to assume that many, if not most, of the findings apply to all loon species until future research reveals otherwise.

Young, inexperienced common loons leave the ocean for the first time when they are two or three years old, returning to the general area where they were raised—on average, thirteen kilometres (8 mi.) from their natal lake, with females dispersing farther than males, some of which settle within two kilometres (1.2 mi.) of the lake where they hatched. Experienced loons, on the other hand, know exactly where they want to settle, and 80 percent of them, both males and females, return to the same territory they occupied the previous season, while the remainder settle in lakes and coves nearby. On average,

^ *Above.* This Arctic Canada landscape, with numerous lakes varying in size and depth, is an ideal habitat for nesting yellow-billed, Pacific, and red-throated loons.

‹ *Opposite.* I hid in a blind to photograph this Pacific loon, which was nesting on a small island about twenty metres (66 ft.) from the shoreline.

a common loon is able to hold on to the same territory for roughly five or six years, although some retain ownership longer. In one case, much longer—a common loon pair in Michigan has returned to the same territory in Seney National Wildlife Refuge for at least twenty-three years! Ultimately, most loons lose their territory to rival intruders, something that may happen to them two or three times in their life. Further details of how this occurs will come later in this chapter.

Returning to a familiar territory year after year carries substantial benefits. A loon knows where a nest was successful and where one may have failed; it knows where prey is located, which predators are a danger, and who its neighbours are—and whether they pose a threat.

Within every breeding population of loons there are three classes of birds: breeding pairs on a territory, nonbreeding pairs on a territory, and birds with no partner and no territory, called *floaters*. Many of the floaters are three- or four-year-old loons who have recently reached sexual maturity and hope to breed for the first time. Normally, floaters roam for a year or two searching for a territory and only breed for the first time when they are, on average, six years old; others may not mate

until they are older, up to eleven years old in one case. In some populations of common loons, the floaters and the territorial nonbreeding pairs may make up nearly half of the entire loon population. By one estimate, only 20 percent of a common loon population produces half of all the chicks.

HOOKING UP

Loons are faithful to their territory but not to their mate. Mated pairs winter separately, sometimes thousands of kilometres apart, and arrive alone or together, depending on whether they happened to reunite in a staging area while waiting for the ice to melt on their nesting lake.

Pioneer loon researcher Judith McIntyre was a keen observer of the common loon and she wrote of their courtship: "For all the spectacular behavior that loons exhibit, such as aggressive combats over territorial rights, night choruses, and ritualized late-summer gatherings, one might expect an equally exciting pattern of courtship behavior. That does not happen. Loon courtship is quiet." Courtship in all loon species is a subdued affair meant to reinforce the pair bond and coordinate their behaviour. While courting, the pairs swim less than half a metre (1.6 ft.) apart,

synchronously dipping their bills and performing simultaneous shallow dives. They circle each other and rub their head on their own shoulder feathers as if they were preening, conspicuously displaying their necklace and throat coloration to their mate.

In the premating period, common loon pairs typically stay within twenty metres (66 ft.) of each other 80 percent of the time, and within visual contact 99 percent of the time. In many bird species, such close attendance is an attempt by the male to monitor his partner in order to prevent her from sneaking a quick mating with an outsider—a clandestine get-together that biologists call an *extra-pair copulation* (EPC). EPCs are especially common in songbirds. Loon researcher Walter Piper wondered

if loons were sometimes unfaithful. Like other birds, a female loon might benefit from an EPC by increasing the genetic variability of her offspring, or by possibly gaining superior genetic qualities from a mate other than her own. As well, an EPC would be a good way for a female to ensure that her eggs would still get fertilized if her mate happened to be sterile. Piper and his colleagues did DNA fingerprinting on fifty-eight chicks from forty-eight different common loon families and found that all were genetic offspring of the parents that raised them. Loons, it seems, were always faithful to their partner.

I have never been lucky enough to witness mating in common loons, but one June in the Canadian Arctic, I watched three different pairs of Pacific loons mate. All loons mate on land, and in the early stages of the breeding season, pairs patrol the shoreline of their nesting lake, prospecting for a suitable nest location, or at least a site where they can easily and safely crawl ashore and mate. One of the Pacific loons I watched crawled ashore, stayed for a couple of minutes while its partner floated nearby, then slipped back into the water, after which the two continued swimming together. I was too far away to hear if they vocalized to each other. In Minnesota, Judith McIntyre reported that either sex of common loon could initiate mating. She observed that roughly half of the time it was the male that climbed ashore first. From the land, he would mew softly and idly pick at vegetation, always keeping his bill pointed to the ground in a nonthreatening position. If the female was interested, the male would slip back into the water and wait for her to climb ashore, then mount her from behind. The male would balance his feet on her shoulders with his head facing forward next to hers; the mating usually lasted less than fifteen seconds, after which the male would immediately dismount by awkwardly clambering forward over his mate's shoulder to reach the water. The female sometimes stayed ashore for up to eight minutes, plucking at vegetation as if building a nest. Copulation sites often become future nest sites, but not always.

The mating pattern I observed in the three pairs of Pacific loons was very similar to that described by McIntyre in the common loon and to what other researchers have documented in yellow-billed and red-throated loons. In red-throated loons, a pair may sometimes build a temporary copulation platform in one of the lakes within their territory, separate from their nesting lake, but this behaviour is infrequent.

^ *Above.* This Pacific loon pair, prospecting for a shoreline nest, swam around this small islet presumably assessing its desirability.

Common loons mate most often in early morning or late afternoon. Researchers assume it doesn't happen at night since loons spend the hours of darkness rafting offshore, where they are safe from shoreline predators. The Pacific loons I watched in the Canadian Arctic were nesting at a latitude where the summer sun never sets. Two of the pairs mated at 8:15 a.m. and 9:25 a.m., and the third pair mated at 2:10 p.m. At this latitude, they may also mate during the evening hours since there is no darkness to conceal potential predators. After a mating session, loons often preen and sometimes bathe.

When it comes to copulatory efforts, mammals reign supreme. For example, ermine may stay coupled for up to two

hours, and one male African lion copulated 157 times in fifty-five hours. Even bonobos, also called pygmy chimpanzees, one of our closest primate relatives, are sexual paragons who copulate repeatedly, not only for reproduction but also to settle disagreements, appease superiors, and to demonstrate affection. Birds, by comparison, are much less athletic in their quest for insemination. To begin with, a male bird doesn't have a penis, although ratites such as the ostrich, emu, and rhea, as well as storks, flamingos, and waterfowl, have a thickening along one wall of their cloaca that can become erect and function like a penis.

Without a penis, how do birds stay linked together long enough for insemination to occur? Loons and other birds have perfected the manoeuvre called the *cloacal kiss*—the cloaca being the terminal portion of a bird's intestinal tract, into which the kidneys and reproductive tracts also empty. During mating, the birds' cloacae pout and kiss for three to six seconds—just long enough for millions of sperm to be passed to the female. Walter Piper estimated that common loons mate roughly half a dozen times during the two weeks prior to egg laying.

❯ *Right.* The water separating this nesting yellow-billed loon from the shoreline was over half a metre (1.6 ft.) deep and may have dissuaded any Arctic fox from predating the nest.

DIY—LOON STYLE

As mentioned earlier, when a prospecting loon is selecting a territory, it has an unconscious checklist of desirable nest-site features. Among them is a shoreline that is not too steep, high, or thickly vegetated, and one where the adjacent water is deep enough to allow for a rapid dive to safety if necessary. The loon also wants a location that has good visibility to watch for predators and trespassing loons—at least 100 to 200 metres (328–656 ft.) for yellow-billed loons—and one that isn't exposed to dangerous waves during stormy weather, or subject to scouring by wind-driven ice.

For all species of loons, an island is the number one choice for a nest location. Sometimes, over 80 percent of all the loons in an area choose island life for their summer home. The islands can range in size from ones larger than a football field to tiny islets barely bigger than a kitchen sink. In the McConnell River area west of Hudson Bay, both Pacific and red-throated loons built "loon-made" islands constructed from mud and aquatic vegetation piled into a mound in shallow water; these islands were located closer to open water than to dry land. Most were less than a square metre (10 sq. ft.) in size, and all were only a few centimetres above the water surface. It seems that any separation a loon can get from the dry shoreline is desirable, as it might yield some protection from land predators, such as Arctic foxes.

A loon builds a nest differently from grebes and penguins, which commonly gather mud and vegetation from a distance and carry it to their nest site. A loon relies solely on materials it can gather in the immediate vicinity of the nest, dredging up mud from the adjacent shallows and tearing out clumps of turf next to it. The size and composition of a loon nest varies greatly. In New England, for example, the nest of a common loon might be a large soggy mound of half-rotten cattails, sedges, mosses, grasses, leaf-litter, and mud dredged from the lake bottom; it might measure up to fifteen centimetres (6 in.) in height and have a diameter of up to 0.9 metres (36 in.)—roughly the size of a roasting pan for a large Christmas turkey—with a shallow bowl at the top to cradle the eggs. Judith McIntyre weighed a nest similar to the one I just described; it tipped the scales at eighteen kilograms (40 lb.). The size of a loon nest naturally varies with the species of loon, with the largest nests usually being built by common loons and the smallest by red-throated loons.

A loon's nest size also depends on the availability of nearby shoreline material. In one study in the rocky Canadian Shield country of northern Saskatchewan, over a quarter of the common loon nests were little more than a slight depression in the soil surface, often with little or no added vegetation. Most of these nests had some overhead covering of willows or alders partially concealing them. Farther north, in the Arctic, with the scarcity of vegetation on the tundra, I have never found a loon nest with any overhead covering, and all were readily visible from a distance. In fact, with binoculars, many could be spotted from more than a kilometre (0.6 mi.) away.

As mentioned earlier, loons are foot-propelled divers; their legs are positioned far to the rear of their bodies, which affects their mobility on land. The esteemed *Oxford English Dictionary* states that the name "loon" is derived from the Old Norse word *lómr*, similar to the modern Swedish and Danish word *lom*, meaning lame, for the awkward walk of the bird on land. Some mistakenly believe the name was derived from the English "lunatic," maintaining that the tremolo call of an agitated common loon resembles the wild laughter of a mentally unstable person. This belief is the origin of the expression

> *Opposite.* The nest of this red-throated loon was a mere depression in the grasses. The owner pulled clumps of soggy turf from the edge of the water and added them to the nest perimeter to fashion a shallow bowl.

"crazy as a loon." The word lunatic is actually derived from the ancient belief that insanity was linked to the phases of the moon. Regardless of the true etymology of the birds' common name, loons are indeed clumsy on land, and consequently, they build their nests as close to the water as possible.

Most loons build their nests at the water's edge or within a metre (3.2 ft.) of the shoreline. A loon virtually never builds a floating nest, as do many grebes, so every loon faces a potential problem. If the water level changes as the season progresses, it could rise and flood the nest, or drop and leave it distant from the water's edge. In spring, when the snow melts, the water level in many northern lakes initially rises. If a nest is built early in the season, it may suddenly be left high and dry in later weeks when the water level drops again. One common loon nest in New Hampshire ended up twenty-six metres (85 ft.) from the water's edge when the lake level dropped. In spite of that, the determined parents successfully hatched their two eggs. In northern Yukon, I monitored a red-throated loon nest that was more than nine metres (29 ft.) from the water's edge. To reach the nest, the incubating loons had to push themselves on their bellies at least a dozen times, occasionally adding a couple of short frog-like jumps.

The opposite problem to stranding is sudden flooding, as might happen if a loon builds its nest on the shore of a reservoir where water levels fluctuate, or if a nesting lake and the surrounding area are suddenly hit with a heavy rainstorm. Most loons can usually accommodate a small, gradual rise in water level of fifteen centimetres (6 in.) or less. By adding material to the nest over two to three days, a pair can keep their nest from flooding. If the increase is greater than this, or if it happens too quickly, the pair will fail. In July 2021, a heavy rainstorm in New Hampshire flooded the nest of a common loon when the lake level rose twenty-three centimetres (9 in.) in twenty-four hours. Experts predict that violent summer storms will increase in frequency as the planet absorbs the full impact of climate change.

Fluctuating water levels aren't always a problem for nesting loons. In Sweden and Finland, Arctic and red-throated loons often build their nests in floating bogs where the mats of sphagnum moss that rim the shoreline adjust naturally to changes in the water level.

Typically, male and female loons cooperate in building a nest, but as in many aspects of loon behaviour, whether that

be incubation, brooding, or chick feeding, there is considerable individual variation, and one partner may do more work than the other. The time it takes to build a nest also varies. In the High Arctic, where loons race to fledge young before freeze-up, speed is necessary, and red-throated loons may build a nest in as little as half a day. In the south, where the nesting season is much longer, a pair of common loons may take a week or more to build a nest, but they can be faster if they get a late start. The meticulous Judith McIntyre timed one pair of common loons that took six hours to build a nest, with their efforts spread over a four-day period. No matter how long a loon pair ultimately takes to build their nest, most continue to add material throughout incubation, dragging in bits of turf and grass to shore up the rim while they dutifully warm the eggs.

The nest location, which is always chosen by the male, is carefully selected, so one would predict that a male would use the same nest in successive years, and indeed they often do. Reuse of the same nest bowl in all loons varies from 30 to 60 percent. When Paul Strong looked at reuse of nests in common loons in Maine and New Hampshire, he found the percentage increased up to 88 percent if he included new nests built

within fifty metres (164 ft.) of old nest bowls. Thus, if an island, a sheltered cove, or a protected peninsula was attractive for nesting in one year, it usually remained so in subsequent years, and even when a pair built a new nest, it was usually in the same general area as their old one. In 2021, a pair of common loons I was following in Alberta built a new nest just two metres (6.6 ft.) away from the nest they had used the previous summer. When I first discovered the new nest, I was surprised to see that two Canada geese had taken over the old loon nest and were incubating a clutch of their own eggs. The geese eventually abandoned their nest. Perhaps having such a close, potentially belligerent, neighbour was too stressful for them to continue.

∧ *Above.* This pair of island-nesting Arctic terns had settled less than ten metres (33 ft.) from a nesting Pacific loon. Whenever I would try to sneak into my photo blind, the terns would betray my approach—and often peck me on the head for good measure.

‹ *Opposite.* The water at the edge of this common loon nest in British Columbia was over sixty centimetres (2 ft.) deep. If danger should threaten, the loon could quietly slip into the water and disappear with barely a ripple, surfacing up to 200 metres (656 ft.) away to distract a predator, and hopefully hide the location of its nest.

^ All species of loons have similar looking nests and eggs. *From upper left:* common loon, red-throated loon, Pacific loon, and yellow-billed loon.

Strong found that a loon's fidelity to an old nest bowl can be quite strong. One pair of common loons he studied in Wisconsin used the same nest four years in a row. In the fifth summer, the nest was saturated and nearly underwater, so the pair built a new nest ten metres (33 ft.) away and laid one egg in it, but they didn't incubate the egg. Ten days later, when the water level had dropped, the pair moved back to their old nest bowl and laid an egg in it, which they immediately began to incubate. Strong retrieved the unincubated egg that had been ignored for ten days and added it to the nest the pair had reoccupied. Surprisingly, both eggs hatched together.

Other birds frequently build their nests on the same islands as those used by nesting loons, and for the same reason—freedom from mammalian land predators. In one Alberta location, neighbouring birds included red-necked grebes, white-winged scoters, lesser scaup, mallards, and American widgeons. In the Arctic, nesting loons commonly share islands with nesting eiders, Sabine's gulls, and Arctic terns. The terns are especially beneficial neighbours as they aggressively mob any imprudent trespasser, and use their sharp, pointed beak to painfully strike polar bears, grizzly bears, caribou, muskoxen, and Arctic foxes, as well as predatory glaucous gulls and jaegers, all of which might pose a danger to the eggs of a nesting loon.

EGG-CITING DETAILS

Once a loon pair has quietly courted and reinforced their bond, fashioned a shallow nest bowl along the shoreline, and mated a handful of times, the female begins to lay. Researcher Keith Yonge, studying common loons in Hanson Lake in northern Saskatchewan, monitored 252 clutches and found that 75 percent of females laid their eggs within a period of nine to twelve days of each other. Such synchrony is more typical of colonial seabirds, such as penguins, which take their cues from the vociferous courtship antics of other colony members to coordinate their

breeding cycle. Yonge wondered if the vocalizations of nesting loons might function similarly to synchronize reproductive events in neighbouring pairs. Although loon pairs might be visually isolated from each other, it is assumed they can hear the calls of neighbours kilometres away.

The peak laying period in every population of loons is closely related to the timing of spring breakup. Most southern loons lay their eggs in May, while species nesting farther north typically delay a month, laying their eggs in June. For example, peak laying of red-throated loons in British Columbia's Gwaii Haanas is in mid-May; along the northern coast of the Yukon, it is June 20; and on Bathurst Island, Nunavut, in the High Arctic, it is June 30.

Since loons are large birds that produce precocious chicks able to swim within a day of hatching, you would expect females to produce relatively large eggs. Naturally, the largest species of loons lay the largest eggs. Both yellow-billed and

common loons lay eggs weighing an average of 146 grams (5.1 oz.), compared to 94 grams (3.3 oz.) for Pacific and Arctic loons, and 78 grams (2.8 oz.) for red-throated loons. One extra-large chicken egg weighs 64 grams (2.3 oz.), less than half the weight of a common loon egg. In her doctoral thesis on the common loon, Judith McIntyre joked, "Anyone who has seen a loon egg is apt to remember it first for its size. Any female loon who has ever laid one no doubt remembers it for the same reason."

I'm addicted to nature trivia, and birds' eggs are a good source of biological minutia. A late friend of mine, Frank Todd, who shared my passion for such trivia, wrote the ultimate source to such bird facts, *10,001 Titillating Tidbits of Avian Trivia*. The smallest bird's egg in the world is laid by the world's smallest bird, the bee hummingbird of Cuba. The hummingbird's egg weighs a mere 0.37 grams (0.013 oz.), and it takes five such eggs to match the weight of a penny. The ostrich occupies the other end of the spectrum and produces the world's largest egg, weighing 1.65 kilograms (3.6 lbs.)—and it's strong enough to support the weight of an adult human standing on it. The largest bird's egg ever found belonged to the extinct elephant bird, which lived in Madagascar. The elephant bird is estimated to have weighed over 450 kilograms (992 lb.) and laid eggs as large as a football. One such egg was estimated to weigh 12.2 kilograms (27 lb.), with a volume equal to that of 180 hen's eggs.

The eggs of all loon species are roughly the same colour, varying from light brown to deep olive with black or dark brown spots. British avian ecologist Tim Birkhead, in his recent book *The Most Perfect Thing: Inside (and outside) a Bird's Egg*, compared the pigmentation process in a bird's egg to an array of paint guns—each gun genetically programmed to fire at a certain time to produce the signature background colour and spotting of a species. An egg normally acquires its colour in the last few hours before it is laid.

Typical of most seabirds, loons produce a small clutch of one or two eggs. The majority of loons may actually produce two eggs, and many reports of one-egg clutches are really just what's left of a two-egg clutch when one of the eggs has been taken by a predator. Three-egg clutches have been reported in

common loons in Minnesota, Wisconsin, Alberta, and British Columbia, but these are extremely rare.

All birds have a compulsory delay between the laying of successive eggs. In loons, one to three days usually separates the laying of the first egg from the second. Incubation does not start in earnest until the second egg is laid, and the first egg is sometimes left uncovered for hours at a time, leaving it vulnerable to predators and lethal overheating or cooling. Earlier, I described a common loon egg in Wisconsin that was left unincubated for ten days but still managed to hatch a healthy chick. The avian embryo is quite resistant to cooling, and generally, nonlethal chilling merely slows its development. In the Arctic, a number of species of shorebirds leave their eggs unattended for up to a week without it resulting in hatching failure, and the same ability to endure cooling may apply to loons.

Should a clutch of eggs disappear—eaten by a predator for example—a female loon may lay a replacement clutch, but it all depends on timing. If the eggs are lost in the first two weeks of incubation, all species of loons may lay again after a compulsory delay of about twelve to fifteen days. If the disappearance occurs in the last half of the incubation period,

> *Opposite.* This red-throated loon was incubating one egg while unexplainably ignoring a second egg lying in the grass beside it. The air temperature at the time was 8°C (46°F), well below the temperature needed for proper embryonic development. After about three hours, the loon's partner took over incubation duties and warmed both eggs.

a female rarely replaces her lost eggs. There may be a couple of reasons for this. For many loons, the nesting season is a critical narrow window, and a late start might not allow enough time to successfully raise chicks to fledging. As well, by the time a female loon has spent several weeks incubating her first clutch of eggs, any additional immature eggs in her ovary may have already started to regress, making reactivation of the process impossible. In the jargon of biology, loons are *determinate egg layers*, which means there is a limit to the maximum number of eggs they can lay in any given nesting season. A rare number of bird species, referred to as *indeterminate egg layers*, will continue to lay until the clutch "feels" right to the incubating female. In a classic experiment conducted in Massachusetts in 1887, Charles Phillips was able to induce a northern flicker (a type of woodpecker) to lay seventy-one eggs in seventy-three days by continually removing eggs from her nest, even though a flicker's usual clutch contains just six to eight eggs. Other species have been fooled into laying way beyond their normal clutch size: 50 eggs in a house sparrow, 128 eggs in a bobwhite quail, and 146 eggs in a mallard. The domestic chicken is certainly the best-known example of an indeterminate egg layer. By artificially selecting hens for egg production, livestock breeders, over hundreds of years, have produced chickens able to lay as many as 352 eggs in 359 days.

INCUBATION—TEDIUM, TENACITY, AND TEAM WORK

All birds' eggs need an external source of heat for development. Most avian embryos require temperatures of at least 37°C (98.6°F) to develop, and when the external air temperature is not high enough to provide that heat, which it rarely is in temperate and polar latitudes, the eggs need to be additionally warmed by a parent bird. This warming behaviour is called *incubation*. In the majority of birds, a few days before a female lays her first egg, some of the feathers on her belly and breast fall out, exposing a bare patch of skin that soon becomes swollen with blood vessels. This so-called *brood patch* is what a bird uses to cover its eggs and warm them. Many seabirds develop a brood patch, but none is found in loons, and I think there may be a good reason for that.

As a patient wildlife photographer, I often spend many hours cramped inside a blind with nothing happening photographically. At times like that, my mind invariably wanders, running ideas through my head to ease the tedium. I had one such moment in Nunavut, in the summer of 2021, when I was in a soggy blind watching a sleepy, red-throated loon incubate its single egg without budging once in two and a half hours. I started to wonder why loons have no brood patch, unlike their closest relatives, the penguins and albatrosses, both of which do. A few seabirds, such as pelicans, boobies, and gannets, also have no brood patch, but they incubate their eggs with the blood flowing in their large webbed feet. Loons have big enough webbed feet to do the same, but they don't use them to incubate, and I suspect they may be too clumsy on land to manoeuvre themselves into position. Could it be that loons have no brood patch because they are the only seabirds that engage in serious, deadly fights, where stabbing injuries to the chest and belly are frequent, and a featherless, vascularized brood patch might make the combatants more vulnerable to a lethal penetration? That's what I concluded while stuck inside the blind, and I'm sticking to that story until someone offers a more plausible explanation. If my speculation is correct, then one might also wonder whether the skin on the chest and abdomen of a loon is thicker than expected, functioning as a dermal shield. I leave that question to be answered by a curious veterinarian. Forty years ago, Judith McIntyre suggested that common loons had increased vascularity in the lower part of their belly that rests on the eggs, and even though their belly is feathered, enough heat leaks through to warm the eggs. This possibility, though plausible, has yet to be studied and confirmed.

The incubation period for all loons ranges from twenty-five to thirty-three days, with the average being around twenty-seven to twenty-nine days. Infertile eggs with no viable embryo inside never hatch, and in rare instances, an adult loon may get fooled into incubating much longer than usual. Scott Sutcliffe had one pair of common loons in New Hampshire incubate an

infertile egg for sixty-six days, and another for a remarkable seventy-four days.

In a case of mistaken identity, a pair of red-throated loons on the north shore of the St. Lawrence River faithfully incubated a worn, spiral-shaped seashell about the size of an egg. Researchers Ron and Hazel Johnson thought the shell may have been accidentally dropped by a gull flying overhead. The researchers removed the shell after watching the loons incubate it for three days "to encourage the faithful pair in a more profitable occupation." Biologist Harry Vogel told me about a common loon in New Hampshire that incubated a tennis ball. The speculation was that the ball had floated over from a nearby boys' camp.

When it comes to sharing incubation duties, loon pairs display a full range of patterns, from the female doing most of the incubation, to equal participation by the male and female, to the female doing relatively little of the nest-sitting duties. In New Hampshire, for example, one loon nest being continuously monitored by webcam revealed that the male incubated for more than 80 percent of the time. Observers suggested that such variability may result when a pair is subjected to unusually oppressive conditions, such as the torment of a blackfly infestation or a stifling heat wave. In these situations, one of the pair may be affected more than the other, which subsequently impacts its tendency to incubate. Age may also be a factor, with inexperienced loons being less committed to incubation than older ones. If there is one generality about the sharing of incubation duties that often seems to apply, it's that male loons tend to incubate more at night and females more during the day.

Typically, loons incubate in shifts ranging from thirty minutes to six hours, but there are reports of stints stretching to thirteen hours in a red-throated loon and more than fourteen hours in one yellow-billed loon. On average, the shifts last around two to four hours. An incubation stint often begins with egg turning and the minor addition of grass bits and turf to the rim of the nest. I've watched many incubating loons start off by facing inland when they first mount the nest. Within a short time, they shift until they are facing the water, presumably so they can readily escape if necessary.

Once an incubation session begins, the loon will often stay in the same position for hours, although it may periodically stand upright with its body tilted at a 45° angle and carefully turn the eggs with its beak before flopping back down again. Some loons

< *Opposite.* A common loon may continue to add sprigs of grass to the edge of its nest throughout the twenty-eight-day incubation period.

are such committed incubators that they may remain on the nest even when a researcher approaches them to check on the eggs. Scott Sutcliffe had to lift a common loon in New Hampshire off its nest to check the egg count, and Jim Richards, a naturalist friend of mine working in Nunavut, had to do the same thing to check on the eggs of an incubating yellow-billed loon.

In Minnesota, one incubating common loon was particularly tenacious in sticking on its nest, becoming a Facebook star in the process. At the time, the bird in question was incubating on an artificial nest raft when a muskrat climbed onto the platform and settled quietly near the loon's head. The odd couple were then joined by a painted turtle that proceeded to crawl onto the loon's back, presumably to be in a higher spot to bask in the sunshine. After sliding off the loon's back a few times, the persistent reptile finally found a spot where it didn't slip. Local photographer Scott Rykken captured the copacetic moment, which he shared on Facebook to the delight of thousands. Rykken said the loon never showed any signs of annoyance, even putting its wing up to keep the turtle from sliding off once it got on top. The chummy terrapin unexpectedly left after ten minutes.

A nest changeover can occur in a number of ways. The incubating bird may wail or mew to solicit its partner. In some instances, the off-duty bird may be so anxious to incubate that it approaches the nest and vocalizes. The incubating bird may also simply leave the nest and join its partner on the water, who then takes over. I witnessed one changeover at a red-throated loon nest in northern Yukon in which the incubating bird mewed softly six or seven times over a fifteen-minute period, after which it left the nest and its mate took over.

Overall, loons keep their eggs covered by one adult or the other more than 90 percent of the time, and this percentage increases the closer they get to the time of hatching. The big exception to this is if a hostile rival invades a pair's territory. The incubating bird will then generally abandon its nest duties to join its mate in confronting the intruder. Unlike grebes and ducks, loons never cover their eggs with nesting material to hide them when they leave, and although loon eggs are camouflaged, they are still easily detected by a gull or jaeger flying overhead. Swedish researcher Magnus Enquist went to Iceland to study how parasitic jaegers search for vulnerable loon eggs. Using artificial nests, gull eggs painted to look like

loon eggs, and several fake red-throated loons made of papier mâché, he discovered the most common method used by jaegers to locate eggs was to memorize the location of each nest in their territory and fly over it periodically to see if it was unprotected. In this study, three-quarters of uncovered eggs were discovered by a patrolling jaeger within an hour, and the remainder within three hours. The jaegers cracked the eggs within seconds of landing, finishing them off within minutes, leaving the empty eggshells in the nest bowl.

One common loon nest I was watching in Alberta had a visitor with a less malign intent. While the incubating loon was absent confronting an intruder, a pair of noisy Canada geese landed in the cove immediately in front of the loon's nest.

⌃ *Above.* The parasitic jaeger, pictured here, and the smaller long-tailed jaeger share their breeding range with many Arctic-nesting loons, whose eggs and chicks they prey upon.

‹ *Opposite.* While incubating, a red-throated loon may turn its eggs every few hours. With its mouth agape, the bird uses the bottom of its lower beak to roll the eggs.

One of the inquisitive geese promptly mounted the vacated nest and stared rather comically at the two large eggs. Having seen a loon kill a trespassing American coot two weeks earlier, I wasn't sure what would happen next. I didn't have to wait long. Within moments, while the goose was still perched on the nest, the returning female loon suddenly surfaced explosively, rushing at the goose, which honked in alarm and narrowly escaped by leaping to the short cattails between my blind and the contested nest. The water was too shallow for the loon to pursue the goose, so it just floated beside its nest, wailing over and over again as if soliciting the help of its male partner, whose only response was to yodel once from the lake. After a minute or so, the agitated female mounted her nest and resumed incubating the eggs. The hapless goose seemed frozen with fright and stayed glued to the security of the cattails only two metres (6.6 ft.) away. The nearness of the goose seemed to unsettle the female, and after a couple of minutes she slid back into the water and swam back and forth menacingly while wailing. I'm certain she would have attacked the goose if it had shifted any closer to her nest or foolishly moved into deeper water. The standoff was broken when the protective mother loon drifted a few metres from her nest. The goose immediately seized the moment, leapt into the air, and noisily escaped to freedom. It would be another thirty minutes before the female finally returned to warm her eggs. The unsettling incident may have temporarily dampened her impulse to incubate, especially since the incident occurred immediately after the agitated pair had just routed out a rival intruder.

BZZZ …

One of the less obvious challenges facing many incubating loons is bloodsucking insects. One summer, I watched an incubating Pacific loon endure an encircling cloud of hungry mosquitoes and wrote these words in my journal: "Out on the tundra beyond the nest, insect life is stirring. In a myriad of puddles and potholes, in the flooded tracks of ATVs, and in a multitude of empty cans carelessly discarded, mosquito larvae are wriggling and about to emerge. Farther south on the banks of fast-flowing rivers, newly surfacing blackflies are lurking in the shadows. Both insects will hungrily torment any incubating loon unluckily tethered to the shoreline."

The tale of the common loon and one particular species of blackfly, with the tongue-twisting name of *Simulium*

euryadminiculum (recently renamed *S. annulus*), is a detective story worth repeating. For the three nature-loving people in North America unfamiliar with the blackfly, it is a small, biting insect whose eggs and larvae develop best in clear, cold fast-running water, which contains an abundance of oxygen. This perfectly describes the conditions in many rivers coursing through the northeastern United States and across boreal Canada. Here, these hump-backed little demons reproduce in numbers that challenge the imagination. In northern Quebec, for example, one rocky outcrop, no larger than a desktop, was covered with 16 million blackfly eggs. When the eggs hatch, the caterpillar-like larvae anchor themselves with silk to the river bottom, where they filter micro-organisms from the currents

^ *Above.* A cloud of blackflies engulfs a brave canoeist paddling in Nunavut, west of Hudson Bay, where both common and Pacific loons nest in summer.

‹ *Opposite.* When a curious Canada goose carelessly mounted a loon nest with eggs in it, the mother loon aggressively drove the goose away.

flowing around them. After a couple of weeks, and six to eight moults, the adults emerge from their silken cocoons and float to the surface on a bubble of gas. Once the little beasts break out of the water and dry their wings, they're ready to rock and roll.

The males and females of all 255 blackfly species in North America feed on plant nectar from flowering trees and shrubs, but the females also relish a meal of blood when they can get one. The female blackfly crudely lacerates the victim's skin with its saw-edged mouthparts, then laps up the blood that oozes into the wound. The nutrients contained in a sanguineous meal are used by the female to provision her eggs, and in many cases, the blood enables her to lay a much larger clutch.

Finding a victim is the first order of business for all bloodthirsty female blackflies. Most follow the scent of carbon dioxide. The concentration of carbon dioxide in exhaled breath can be 150 times greater than it is in the atmosphere, and insects have sensors in their antennae that can detect the gas from as much as eighty metres (87 yd.) downwind. Typically, the insects fly upwind in a zigzag course that holds them in the odour plume and systematically moves them closer to their quarry. In the 1960s, Canadian entomologists J. Lowther and Donald

Wood observed *Simulium annulus* in Ontario's Algonquin Park skipping along the water surface. They believed the blackflies were searching in the air over the water not only for telltale carbon dioxide but also for the volatile odours released by the uropygial oil gland of the common loon. To confirm that the oil gland secretions were an olfactory cue for the blackfly, Lowther and Wood ran a series of tests using museum skins of a common merganser (a fish-eating duck), a pied-billed grebe, and a herring gull, plus the skin of a freshly killed common loon. When all the skins were placed together on a beach, the blackfly species being studied was only attracted to the dead loon.

Lowther and Wood suspected that the blackflies initially locate a loon by chemical means but then rely on visual clues from the head and neck plumage to select a target area. Roughly fifty years later, Wisconsin biologist Meggin Weinandt and a trio of colleagues set out to prove that point. The imaginative researchers used decoys, fitted with wings from a deceased loon, and attached glueboards to the top of the decoys' heads and immediately in front of their tails to trap any blackflies they lured. The scientists concluded that the blackfly *Simulium annulus* was indeed attracted to the chemical signals from the loon's plumage and specifically targeted the neck and head of the bird. They also confirmed that it was the only blackfly species that regularly fed on common loons.

Blackfly outbreaks are typically linked to cool spring weather and usually last just three weeks in May. The neck feathers of heavily bitten loons are conspicuously ruffled, perhaps the result of the underlying skin being swollen from numerous bites. Researcher Walter Piper observed incubating loons in Wisconsin during a blackfly outbreak and counted the number of head shakes the birds made in their efforts to dislodge the bloodthirsty flies. In the first week of an outbreak in May, the loons made 7.8 head shakes per minute; in the second week, 3.2; in the third week, 3.1; and in the fourth week, just 0.4 head shakes per minute. The loons made no head shakes in the weeks afterwards, once the blackfly numbers had greatly declined.

Piper wondered what impact the blackfly harassment would have on a loon's breeding success. He looked at twenty-four years of data, and his findings were startling. In those years when blackfly numbers were high, loons were more apt to abandon their nest; the birds spent less time incubating, and the number of two-chick families declined. He thought the

reason for fewer two-chick families was because the tormenting flies disrupted incubation, compelling some adults to abandon their nest after the first egg hatched. Over the twenty-four-year period, Piper thought the nest abandonments caused by blackflies reduced the annual number of fledglings by an average of 6.1 percent per year.

Bloodthirsty mosquitoes can sometimes be as bothersome to an incubating loon as blackflies. Both insects have a similar life history, and in mosquitoes, as in blackflies, only the females feed on blood. No one has studied whether the bloodthirsty plague of "mozzies" that sweep across the Arctic tundra every summer impacts the breeding success of the loons that nest there. Nonetheless, I have watched multiple nesting loons contend

with the scourge of mosquito season, repeatedly shaking their head and snapping at their insect tormentors, now and then actually catching one and swallowing it. I've never been able to tell if a mosquito can penetrate a loon's thick plumage the way a blackfly can, and I have only been able to watch them target a bird's unfeathered eyelids and the bare skin at the base of its beak. One July, in Nunavut, I was photographing a Pacific loon nest when the incubating pair changed over. When the new bird mounted the nest, a cloud of hundreds of mosquitoes erupted from the grass beside it. After thirty-five minutes of torment, the bird unexpectedly left the nest and began to scratch its face repeatedly, after which it preened vigorously for seventeen minutes. While preening, the loon repeatedly shook its head, often with its mouth agape, something I had never seen during any preening session before. It was hard not to surmise that the bird was itchy from repeated insect bites.

EGG SNATCHERS

With all the hurdles facing an incubating pair of loons, it's no surprise that many eggs never hatch, no matter how committed the birds may be. Biologist Keith Yonge, working in Saskatchewan's Hanson Lake in the early 1980s, followed the fate of 428 common loon eggs from 252 nests. In his study, only 38 percent of the eggs hatched. In a Minnesota study, the success rate was 43 percent, and in an Alberta study, it was 70 percent. The hatching rate in Pacific loons nesting in northern Yukon varied from 92 percent down to just 28 percent. Red-throated loons nesting in the same area of the Yukon had hatching success varying from 33 percent up to 78 percent.

In Saskatchewan, Yonge summarized the fate of the 265 eggs in his study that never survived to hatching: 5.4 percent were infertile, 3.5 percent were knocked from the nest, 4.3 percent were abandoned, 13.9 percent were washed out of the nest, 16.8 percent were taken by predators, and 17.7 percent mysteriously disappeared, although he felt many may have been predated. Of the eggs taken by predators, 82 percent were eaten by ravens and herring gulls and 18 percent by mink.

In every study of loon hatching success, predators play a major role in whether a nesting season succeeds or fails. The egg snatchers come in two flavours, avian and mammalian. Examining a predated nest can help a loon researcher decide who the culprit was. If the eggshells have a hole in them, the

predator was most likely a bird, possibly a herring gull or a parasitic or long-tailed jaeger. One time on Victoria Island, Nunavut, I watched an adult red-throated loon guard its eggs from a pair of parasitic jaegers. The loon defended its clutch from the water and would aggressively rush the jaegers each time one of them tried to land on the nest. After repeatedly failing, the egg thieves finally flew away.

Some of the largest avian predators have a wide enough gape to pick up a whole loon egg and fly off with it. There is a report from northern Ontario of a common raven flying directly towards an incubating common loon, which slipped off its nest as the bird approached. The loon offered no resistance when the raven

∧ *Above.* The cunning and adaptable Arctic fox influences the nesting biology and success of more Arctic birds than any other mammalian predator.

‹ *Opposite.* When this Pacific loon climbed onto its nest to incubate, it caused a cloud of bloodthirsty mosquitoes to erupt from the grass. Now and then, it would catch one of its insect tormentors and eat it.

landed, picked up a whole egg, and flew away. In the Arctic, the glaucous gull, one of the world's largest species of gulls, was seen carrying off a whole yellow-billed loon egg in its beak. Both the raven and the glaucous gull can easily carry away the eggs of the smaller loon species, leaving no evidence of their thievery.

All of the major avian predators patrol shorelines to scavenge for dead fish, and it's likely they soon learn the location of any nesting loons, and probably monitor the nests for unattended eggs. Despite the size and intimidating demeanour of these avian thieves, most loons can successfully fend them off when they are sitting on their nest. A loon's sharp beak is a dangerous weapon and one to be respected by any prospective egg-napper.

Some avian egg predators are just too big for a loon to challenge. In the McConnell River area west of Hudson Bay, sandhill cranes were an unexpected predator on the nests of Pacific and red-throated loons. In Wisconsin, where nesting bald eagles are now more abundant than in years gone by, biologist Kyle McCarthy reported on four different instances of eagles eating loon eggs. In one case, an immature eagle spent over seventeen minutes eating an egg, despite the adult loon swimming back and forth in front of it, wailing repeatedly.

Every nesting loon must contend with at least one predatory mammal with an appetite for eggs. In the south, raccoons probably pose the biggest threat. These masked bandits thrive in human-modified environments where overflowing garbage cans and friendly cottage owners encourage their presence. Typically, raccoons forage along shorelines, so they would naturally encounter nesting loons and eagerly predate any eggs they found.

In the Arctic, grizzly bears and wolves may occasionally eat a loon egg, but when it comes to nest raiding, none can compete with the cunning Arctic fox. The fox is a highly adaptable carnivore, scavenging seal carcasses killed by polar bears on the sea ice and tirelessly searching for lemmings, birds' eggs, and nestlings on the tundra. When lemming numbers are low, as they are in a cyclical fashion, the foxes switch their focus to the eggs of waterfowl and loons. One year, on Alaska's Seward Peninsula, the Arctic foxes, with the help of local red foxes, destroyed 83 percent of the red-throated loon nests. The following year, the predatory vulpine duo wiped out 72 percent of nests.

A nesting loon, of any species, has no hope of defending its eggs from a hungry fox. Their best defence is to nest on an

> *Opposite.* This red-throated loon adopted a hangover posture in response to the sudden appearance of a shaggy muskoxen, which posed no threat to the loon or its eggs.

inaccessible island or avoid detection if they have chosen a vulnerable shoreline location. When an incubating loon first spots a hunting fox, it immediately slumps down and drapes its neck over the edge of the nest. This is a defensive posture biologists call a *hangover pose*, which indicates the bird is preparing to escape. If the fox continues to come closer, the loon may noiselessly slip into the water, barely leaving a ripple, and surface up to 200 metres (219 yd.) away in an attempt to distract the fox and hide the location of its nest. If the clever fox still finds the nest, the agitated loon may call excitedly and perform a dramatic *penguin display*, in which it noisily treads water in front of the predator. The defensive loon's splashing behaviour rarely dissuades a hungry fox, which typically carries the eggs away, one at a time, to be eaten elsewhere or cached for the future.

LOON TUNES

The wail is one of the four distinctive calls given by adult common loons. Often described as melancholic, haunting, and ghostly in nature, the wail has sometimes been mistaken for the plaintive howl of a wolf. William Barklow, who studied

> *Right.* When a common loon wails, its throat swells and its bill remains closed or slightly open.

loons in Maine in the 1970s, poignantly described the wail as a sound "detached from the earth." Loon vocalizations have been studied most intensively in the common loon, and the following discussion revolves around those studies.

The wail is primarily a long-distance contact call, often given when one member of a pair is looking for its partner or when an adult is searching for a chick it can't find. It is a request for closer contact or assistance, and it may be audible more than a kilometre (0.6 mi.) away. Recall the example I described earlier of a distressed, incubating female loon repeatedly wailing to her partner, summoning him, when a Canada goose had mounted their nest.

The *wail* is a simple, graded call with no complex harmonics, varying from one to three notes in length. As the number of notes increases, the pitch, or frequency, increases, starting at around 650 hertz and increasing up to 1,140 hertz. The higher the frequency, the greater the graveness of the situation, and the more the caller is pleading for contact. (For readers interested in hearing the different loon calls, I highly recommend the Loon Preservation Committee's website, https://loon.org/the-call-of-the-loon/.)

The *hoot* is the simplest of the loon's four basic calls. It is a soft, abbreviated vocalization used primarily for short-range communication to maintain contact between family members or among the birds in a small flock. The pitch can vary somewhat depending on mood and circumstance, a reflection that communication between loons is often subject to subtle nuance.

The *tremolo* is another long-distance call. It has been likened to a wild, agitated laugh. It is the call familiar to anyone who has accidentally paddled near the nest of a loon or a family with chicks. It is a vocalization given when the caller is distressed, perhaps frightened by a predator, an intruding loon, or a human boater. Like the wail call, the tremolo is a graded

vocalization that biologists categorize as tremolo Type I, Type II, and Type III, which vary in frequency from 600 to 2,000 hertz. Once again, the higher the frequency, the more troubled and agitated is the caller.

The tremolo is typically the only call a common loon ever gives when flying, although researchers have on rare occasions heard a loon yodel in flight. Researcher William Barklow noted that, in 90 percent or more of cases, any time a loon flew over a lake that was occupied by a territorial pair, the flyer would give a tremolo call. The occupying pair did not always respond, but when they did, it was often with a yodel. I will explain the reason for this in a moment.

A mated pair may sometimes perform a tremolo duet. The pair call at different frequencies which, with practice, can sometimes be detectable by a human listener. The actual purpose of the duet is unclear, but the calling may reinforce the pair's bond. Duets are more common in newly formed pairs and may help the individuals become familiar with each other's calls.

The last of the four basic loon vocalizations is the *yodel*, which, like the wail and the tremolo, is meant for long-distance communication. Biologist Sigurd Olson called it "blood-

curdling and maniacal, but thrilling and beautiful." The yodel differs from other loon calls in that it is only given by male loons, and each male has his own unique signature yodel, like a vocal fingerprint. The average listener, without experience, can normally not detect the auditory subtleties of a male's yodel, and researchers measure the uniqueness of a yodel by converting it into a sound spectrogram, which is a graphic representation of the frequencies of the call as it varies over time.

The yodel is the common loon's most structurally complex vocalization. It consists of an introductory phrase followed by a variable number of two-syllable repeating units. Yodels are a vocal proclamation of territorial ownership and are given most often when an intruder invades a male's territory, or in response to the tremolo call of a loon flying overhead. Barklow called the yodel a male's attack message, conveying an aggressive intent.

Researcher Jay Mager believes a yodelling male transmits three kinds of information when he calls. First, it identifies who the caller is, as each male has his own unique yodel pattern. Second, because of the frequency and timing characteristics of the introductory phrase of the call, which scientists can measure on a computer, it relays an honest signal of health and body size. The frequency of the introductory phrase is influenced by the anatomy of the vocal tract, namely the size and shape of the bird's trachea and voice box (syrinx), which correlate with its body size. It is a cue that the caller cannot fake. Mager and others have learned that the body weight of a male loon may vary from year to year, and as its weight varies, so does the frequency of its yodel. It is assumed that a bigger body weight indicates a healthier bird and one better able to fight and defend his territory. And finally, the third piece of information conveyed in a yodel is the male's level of motivation, which is reflected in the number of repeating units, which varies from one to nine, added to the end of the call. The more repeating units there are, the higher the male's willingness to fight and escalate a confrontation.

Males yodel most frequently when they first return to their territories in spring, and then again just before their eggs hatch. In the first instance, the newly arriving yodeller is vocally staking his claim on a valuable piece of real estate. In the second instance, the male, after investing roughly four weeks in maintaining ownership of the family territory during the lengthy incubation period, wants to deter intruders that

‹ *Opposite.* When a male common loon yodels, it often pivots in the water, sending the sound spraying out across the lake.

might endanger the lives of his newly hatched chicks, since it's fairly common for intruders to kill chicks.

When a loon flies over a territory and tremolos, it may trigger the occupying male to respond with a yodel. The intent of the flyer is to assess the fighting ability and motivation of the owner. Basically, it's collecting information to evaluate the risk of attempting to take over the territory, and whether such a bold intrusion would be too dangerous and result in failure, or worse, serious injury or death. In response to the tremolo of a flying loon, a small male on a territory may be more reluctant to yodel than a larger one because it would betray his diminished body weight and physical fitness. However, when they do yodel, they often include more repeating units, suggesting they are highly motivated to confront and fight an intruder despite their smaller size.

As just outlined, each of the four vocalizations occurs primarily in response to specific social circumstances. The nocturnal chorus is the exception to this generality. At night, it's possible for a listener to hear the full loon repertoire in a relatively short length of time. In Michigan, researcher Lauren Wentz studied the who, when, what, and why of these nocturnal choruses. The participants in these choruses were variable. On whole-lake territories, the occupying pair were usually the sole singers, but on lakes with multiple territorial pairs, adjoining neighbours would usually participate. More neighbours produced more choruses.

Most often, a chorus began with wails, and Wentz recorded these distinctive calls in 92 percent of the sing-alongs. The next most frequent calls were yodels, which occurred in 71 percent of the choruses, as compared to 66 percent for tremolos and 46 percent for tremolo duets. The average nocturnal chorus lasted just three to four minutes, and successive choruses were usually separated by roughly one to two hours. The choruses occurred mainly in the early part of the nesting season, peaking just prior to the average egg-laying date in May, and occurred primarily in the early hours of darkness, and then again near sunrise, although loons might vocalize anytime throughout the night.

When calling at night, the birds were not busy and distracted with feeding, nest duties, and patrolling their territories. As well, there is less background noise at night from wind and waves, making transmission favourable for long-range communication. Wentz found that 98 percent of nocturnal choruses occurred when the wind speed was less than eight kilometres per hour (5 mph). Additionally, the nighttime calling loons had fewer other species producing sounds in the same frequency ranges, although barred, great grey, and great horned owls sometimes call in the 1,000 to 2,000 hertz range, which overlaps with the frequencies used by calling loons.

The question that is still unanswered is, what function do nocturnal choruses serve? Are they simply to see which loons are in the neighbourhood, and whether all neighbouring territories are occupied by healthy owners? Or is it an evaluation exercise to learn which territories are weakly defended, offering the potential for territorial expansion or takeover by the participants? The questions remain.

The above discussion focused on the calls of the common loon, as they are the most studied species in the family; yet, all loons are highly vocal on their nesting grounds. The yellow-billed loon, the common loon's closest relative, has virtually the same repertoire and uses its calls in the same way, although its vocalizations are slightly lower in frequency and delivered more slowly. The Pacific and Arctic loons wail and yodel but replace the tremolo call with growls and croaks. Canadian

ornithologist and explorer Dewey Soper, working in Baffin Island in the late 1920s, wrote of the Pacific loon, "Its lonely wail was almost constantly heard floating with dismal insistence on the varying winds of the tundra—the most melancholy voice of the Arctic lands." The red-throated loon, the most ancestral member of the family, has a repertoire of up to nine calls, which contrasts with the other loon species, all of which have just four basic calls. The red-throated loon does not yodel. In place of this distinctive territorial vocalization, a pair of red-throats does a territorial duet that seems to serves a similar function.

HOSTILE TAKEOVERS

Recall that eight out of ten breeding loons return to the same nesting territory they used the previous season, and they retain ownership of that territory for an average of five to six years. Scientists now know that a common loon may hold two or three different territories in its lifetime, and many of these territorial changes come after conflict, eviction, and takeover. Until the early 1990s, when the colour-banding of adult loons began in earnest, researchers could not identify individual loons, so they usually had no idea whether an adult was always pairing with

the same partner, or whether pairs on a territory were long-standing occupants or new arrivals. Once individuals could be reliably identified, the fluid nature of territorial occupancy was revealed, and the details are surprisingly complex.

Early in the breeding season, there is an inevitable scramble for birds to occupy a territory. Once a pair claims a territory, the challenge doesn't end there, as they must then continually defend the territory from intruders wishing to evict them. These intruders, both males and females, may be young birds with no breeding experience, birds which bred in the past but were evicted from or abandoned a previous territory, or in rare instances, breeders that have a territory and are prospecting for a better one. These are the birds described earlier that fly over an occupied territory and give a tremolo call, attempting to evaluate the strength and commitment of the owner. Among common loons, intrusions occur between two and five times per day, peaking during the chick-rearing period. Intruders are not just interested in the attributes of the territory owners and whether they can be overpowered and ousted, they also want to know if the territory is productive enough to raise chicks. Often, an intruder will have flown over a territory the

> *Opposite.* A resident common loon expels an intruder in a lengthy wing-rowing chase.

previous summer on a reconnaissance flight and seen that the owners had chicks. This discovery would greatly increase the territory's desirability. In fact, researchers have shown that when a territory has produced young one year, the number of intrusions increases by 60 percent the following year.

An intrusion begins either when a trespasser lands on a whole-lake territory or one swims across the boundary of a partial-lake territory. Once this happens, the owners quickly converge and confront the intruder—males challenging males, females challenging females. The trio may start by swimming in circles and engaging in a series of brief dives. From there, the confrontation may escalate to splash dives and wing-rowing chases around the territory. I watched one exhausting chase that lasted over five minutes, during which the birds circled the perimeter of the small lake four times—the lead bird repeatedly giving agitated tremolo calls.

In the common loon, a takeover attempt will often last twenty minutes or more before the outsider is finally expelled. One prolonged confrontation went on for ninety-three minutes and ended with the eviction of the owner. In red-throated loons, territorial intrusions are usually terminated in less than ten minutes. If the resident pair is already incubating, the trespasser is frequently ousted in just two to three minutes. If the pair has chicks, then the eviction is even faster, with the intruder aggressively chased away in less than a minute.

Most takeover attempts conclude with a minimum of aggression, ending when the intimidated outsider flies away. In a minority of cases, however, the trespasser stays and the interaction escalates to fighting. Loons may fight by launching a surprise underwater attack, by stabbing their adversary in the chest or belly, or by lunging at their opponents, grappling with their beaks and beating each other with their heavy wings. They use their dagger-shaped bills to stab and grab, and they force their rival's head underwater. I witnessed one protracted fight between two males and was surprised by the hapless determination of the apparent intruder. It was early spring in the foothills of Alberta's Rocky Mountains, and I was hidden in a photo blind on the shore of a lake still half covered with ice. A pair of loons was swimming in the ice-free water at the south end of the lake, and a third loon was foraging in a sliver of open water in front of my blind. Suddenly, one of the paired birds surfaced near the foraging loon and began to viciously attack

it. Each combatant grabbed the other's facial feathers with his stiletto beak, while at the same time they pummelled each other with their powerful, heavy wings. The attack lasted less than a minute before one of the loons, which I thought was the foraging bird, suddenly dove and disappeared. The attacking loon left soon afterwards and swam back to his partner. I was mystified as to how the foraging loon had miraculously escaped, and where it had gone. Ten minutes later, I got my answer. With his rival gone, and the danger past, the missing loon suddenly flapped out from his hiding place in a cluster of cattails. He was missing some feathers from the top of his head and the nape of his neck, and he had a bleeding cut at the base of his lower bill, but otherwise seemed okay. He preened vigorously for several minutes then flapped his wings twice, which I assumed was intended to settle his ruffled and dishevelled plumage. For some unexplained reason, after being aggressively attacked and forced to flee into a thicket of cattails, the injured loon began to wail, calling at least twenty times. It seemed like a clear taunt to the resident pair swimming 300 metres (328 yd.) away. The calls did not go unnoticed or unchallenged. The resident male responded quickly to the loon's boldness and immediately

‹ *Opposite.* When a Pacific loon assumes the vulturine posture similar to the wing display of the New World vultures (Cathartidae), it is communicating its highly agitated state and readiness to attack.

attacked the wailing bird for a second time. The attacked bird, which I assumed was an unwelcome intruder, wasn't foolish enough to try fighting again and instead attempted to escape from his assailant by flapping across the top of some thin ice, but his frantic efforts caused the ice to break and fragment. The imprudent bird clearly did not feel safe on the broken ice and at the first opportunity fled to the cattails again, closely chased by his aggressive rival. The two birds briefly stabbed at each other and clubbed with their wings before the intruder, once again, was able to escape into the cattails beyond the reach of his adversary, who swam menacingly back and forth along the edge of the shore. After a couple of minutes, the victor yodelled and swam back to his mate. The defeated intruder was still hidden in the cattails when I left thirty minutes later. Biologists report similar instances where a defeated loon escapes to shore, rests for a time, then safely flies away, which is how I hoped this interaction eventually concluded.

Not all takeover attempts have such a relatively happy ending. In 15 percent of them, the resident male is evicted, and of those males, up to a third of them are killed by the victorious intruder. After thinking about it for some time, I wondered if the intruder in my story was actually the original owner of the territory, and the fights I saw were him being evicted from his old territory by a new male. That would explain his apparent stubbornness and persistence in remaining on the lake after he was soundly beaten and forced to escape into the cattails twice. The loons were unbanded and unknown to me, so I don't know if this explains what happened, but it's possible.

Lethal combat is relatively rare in animals, and biologists were surprised to discover that a territorial male loon would sometimes fight to the death to retain his territory. Veteran researcher Walter Piper, who has studied loon takeovers extensively, suggested that maybe only older males with declining body condition would fight with such intensity. He called this his "desperado hypothesis." An old male may have only a few reproductive years remaining, and by desperately risking death, he hopes to retain his familiar territory for another year or two instead of being evicted and displaced. Piper suggested that old males may invest less energy in staying alive and more energy in reproduction because they have less to lose. The hypothesis is unproven but remains a tantalizing explanation.

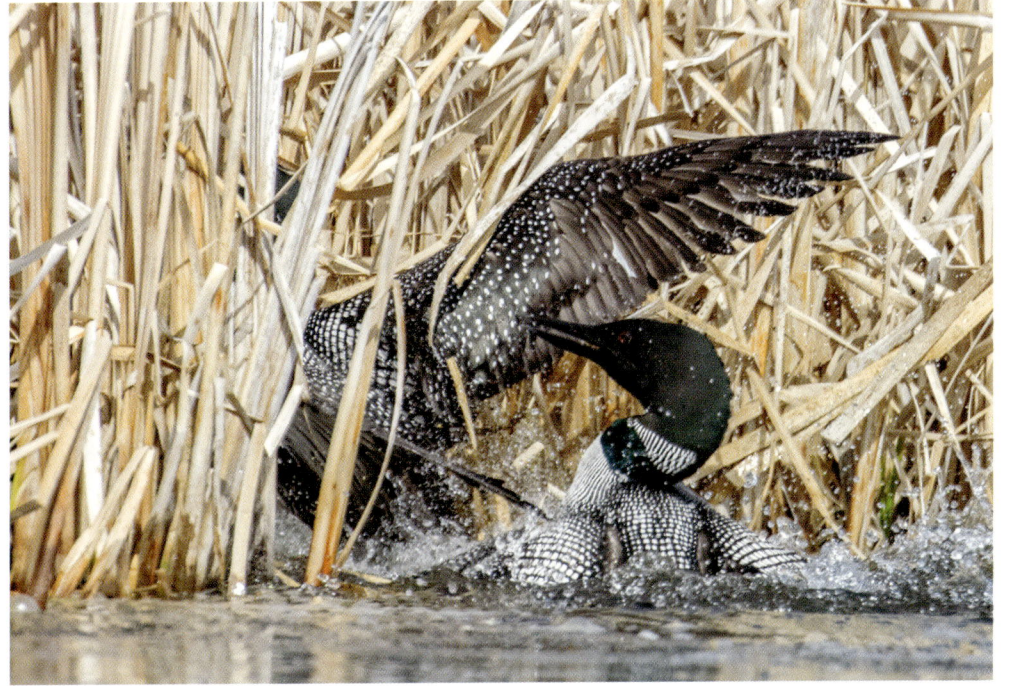

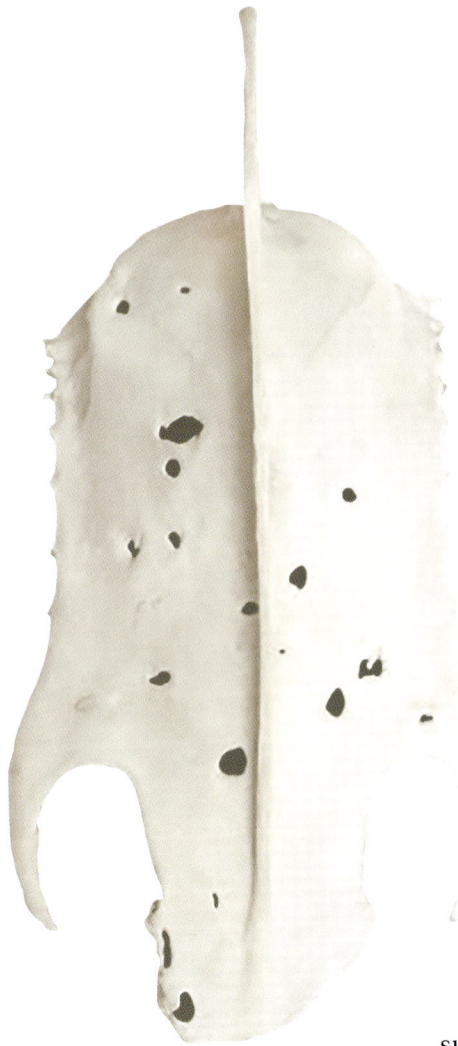

∧ *Above.* Sternal punctures are a common injury in fighting loons. This sternal specimen has seventeen holes in it.

The frequency of vicious fighting was largely unsuspected by biologists, but Mark Pokras, a veterinarian and professor emeritus at Tufts University, had done hundreds of necropsies on dead loons, and he knew better. In a 2021 paper, coauthored with Amanda Higgins and Meghan Hartwick, Pokras chronicled sternal punctures in common loons. Over the eight years of the study, more than half of the 574 loons they examined each had an average of seven sternal punctures. The most surprising discovery was that there was no difference in the number or severity of sternal punctures between males and females, and that both sexes likely engaged in serious fights many times in their life. Although both sexes typically had between three and eleven sternal punctures, one of the males had twenty-four, and one of the females had seventeen. Field biologists had always suggested that serious battles with stabbing wounds only occurred between rival males. The incidence of multiple sternal punctures in females clearly suggests otherwise. It's still unknown why there are so few reports of female fights.

The authors suggested it may simply be that females are more secretive and silent during such serious interactions.

What happens to the displaced breeders once they are driven from their territory? As already stated, up to a third of evicted males die from lethal wounds sustained in the takeover. Evicted females, it seems, rarely fight so fiercely that they are killed. According to Walter Piper, studying in northern Wisconsin, most displaced loons, including both males and females that survive eviction, move to vacant lakes nearby and behave like floaters, wandering about and intruding into a variety of lakes in the vicinity of their former territory. Five of the loons he was following (three females and two males) established new territories between 0.2 and 5.4 kilometres (0.12 to 3.4 mi.) of their old stomping grounds. Some even reclaimed their old territory after mounting a hostile takeover of their own.

Piper was also interested in what happens to the opposite pair member when there was a takeover. He learned that, in some cases, both pair members became takeover victims within six weeks of each other. In 21 percent of the pairs, the victorious intruder mated with the remaining partner and produced chicks. And in those instances when a male takeover occurred

❯ *Right.* This female loon had fresh blood on her breast and belly from a fight with another female. The circled area on the edge of the nest contained a large amount of clotted blood, indicating that the injury was not a trivial one.

in a territory with chicks, the chicks were invariably killed by the intruder despite the female attempting to defend them.

One final thought about takeovers. Recall that each male loon has a distinctive yodel. In a fascinating 2006 paper entitled "Changing Territories, Changing Tunes," researchers Charles Walcott, Jay Mager, and Walter Piper reported that when a male loon takes over a new territory, he substantially changes the introductory phrase of his yodel, and that the magnitude of the change was greater than the normal year-to-year variation that might occur if his body weight changed, equal in magnitude to the difference between different loons. They concluded that a male loon has considerable flexibility in its vocalizations and is not constrained to a single, fixed yodel. It seems, when a newcomer revises his yodel, he does it to be as different as possible from the previous resident, basically asserting that he is "the new loon on the lake."

CHAPTER 6

Loonling Life: The Race to Make It Aloft

On June 16, 2020, I was inside my photo blind by 6:45 a.m. I had spent over a hundred hours in the previous three weeks observing this particular incubating pair of common loons, and I expected their eggs to hatch within three to five days. When I arrived, the female seemed uneasy. She was facing away from me and her rump jerked upwards three or four times. I wondered if there was a chick or two squirming under her. She wailed plaintively and looked around. Was she summoning her partner, who was floating quietly at the mouth of the family nesting cove? At that moment, a helicopter started to circle high above the lake, and the male responded by yodelling eleven times in a row, the most frequent I had ever heard any male yodel. The female's rump jerked upwards again six or seven times in a matter of a minute, and she hooted. I couldn't understand what was happening. Was she simply adjusting her legs to be more comfortable around the eggs, or was there a chick hatching beneath her?

Two hours later, I got the answer when a tiny downy chick appeared briefly under her right wing. Another hour passed, and there was a loud splash at the mouth of the cove. The female stretched her neck as high as possible, as if trying to see what had caused the noise. I wondered if it wasn't one of the local beavers that share the lake with the loons, but it turned out to be a pair of noisy canoeists. When she spotted them, the loon immediately slipped off the nest. For the next three-quarters of an hour, I watched the newly hatched loonling explore the nest alone. Periodically, it pecked and tugged enthusiastically at some sprigs of dried grass, and as it did, it peeped faintly. The temperature was just 7°C (45°F), and the wind was cool. I worried that the vulnerable chick might get hypothermic, or worse, be spotted by a hungry raven flying overhead.

When the mother finally returned, the male conveniently yodelled from the lake confirming that it was indeed the female who was back on the nest. The male had done no incubating in the six hours since I had arrived. As the mother loon mounted the nest, she seemed to ignore the black, downy chick huddled at the edge, and focused solely on positioning the remaining unhatched egg under her belly. The overlooked chick pecked at its mother's wing with its tiny beak, and the female reflexively lifted her wing so the chick could move underneath. When the loonling finally disappeared, I could still hear it peeping under the female's body. After some time, the chick's head appeared

< *Opposite.* This common loon was still incubating an unhatched egg when the first chick hatched. When the chick got cold and needed to warm up, it would peck on its parent's wing and move underneath.

PHOTO BLIND

NESTING LOON

under the front of its mother's wing, and it once again tugged at some dried grasses, rested for a time, then tugged some more before snuggling under its mother.

Another hour passed, and suddenly there were two chicks under the female's wing—one by her head and the other near her tail. Both, intermittently and repeatedly, did the familiar grass-tugging, pecking, and resting routine. I had been cramped inside the blind for over eight hours, but I had finally witnessed the behaviour I had hoped to see of newly hatched chicks in the early moments before the family abandoned their nest. I left without disturbing them.

GET CRACKING

As discussed earlier, most common loons in southern Canada and the adjacent United States lay their eggs in May, and after being incubated for roughly twenty-eight days, the eggs hatch in June. Farther north, the common loons nesting in Canada, Alaska, and Greenland, as well as most Pacific, red-throated, and yellow-billed loons, delay the cycle by a month, with the majority laying their eggs in June, with chicks hatching throughout July and sometimes into early August.

Every hatchling is equipped with an egg tooth—a hard, sharp projection on the tip of its upper beak that it uses to free itself from the shell. The chick must wiggle, kick, squirm, stretch, and chip its way to freedom without any help from its parents. The power for its first pecks comes from a specialized hatching muscle on the rear of its neck. The muscle later atrophies, and the egg tooth disappears by the time the young loons are two weeks old. Once the shell begins to crack, called *starring*, it usually takes the loon chick a day or two to finally break free.

Young loon chicks can be heard calling from inside the egg, sometimes as much as four days before they hatch. At one Pacific loon nest I was watching along the western coast of Hudson Bay, the first chick hatched more than twenty-four hours before its sibling did. Twice, the parent bird swam away from the nest with its newborn chick and left the second egg uncovered. From my blind fifteen metres (50 ft.) away, I could hear the chick inside the egg continuously chirping. At one point, the adult, with the hatchling close beside it, was foraging more than 100 metres (109 yd.) away from its nest. The adult seemed oblivious to the chick calling from the unattended egg.

❮ *Opposite.* From the photo blind on the shore of this cattail cove, I spent over 100 hours observing a pair of incubating common loons in the foothills of the Rocky Mountains.

After fifteen minutes, the parent slowly returned to the nest, and as it rolled the egg under its body, I could see that one end had cracked open— the chick would soon wiggle its way to freedom. The following day, both chicks were swimming with the adults.

Newly hatched birds vary dramatically in their preparedness for life outside the egg. Hatchling American robins and eastern bluebirds, for example, are naked and blind, have no ability to warm themselves, and are totally dependent on their parents for food. In contrast, the chicks of shorebirds and grouse are well-developed little hatchlings covered with downy plumage. They can run about and feed themselves as soon as they hatch, and they can generally control their body temperature. Biologists use the terms *altricial* and *precocial* to describe the two ends of this developmental spectrum. Newly hatched loon chicks are an intermediate blend of the two and are referred to as *semiprecocial*, as their parents must initially feed them and also brood them when temperatures are cool.

When a loon chick first hatches, it looks soggy and pitiful. Its down is wet and matted, but within an hour or two, the chick transforms into a photogenic little fluffball. Hatchling

Pacific, Arctic, and red-throated chicks sport a thick greyish-brown down on their heads and backs, while their breasts and undersides are a pale grey. Yellow-billed and common loon chicks are slightly sootier in colour and have a pale breast and whitish belly. All loon chicks go through two downy coats. The second coat appears when the hatchlings are just two to three weeks old and is somewhat browner in colour.

Recall that most loon eggs are laid one to three days apart. Typically, incubation begins after the first egg is laid, but it may initially be sporadic, varying from a few minutes each day up to 50 percent of the time. As a result, the two eggs hatch at different times, usually one to two days apart. After the first chick hatches, the empty eggshell may get crushed and trampled into the nest. More often, however, a parent swims away with it and drops it to the lake bottom, five to ten metres (16 to 33 ft.) away from the nest. The inside of a loon eggshell is bright white in colour and can easily be seen from a distance. Removing it may keep the remaining egg from being detected by a predator.

In common loons, the family usually abandons the nest within a day of the second egg hatching. In contrast, Pacific, Arctic, and red-throated loon families may continue to use the

nest to brood their chicks, but only for three or four more days. In all species of loons, once a chick is finally led from the family nest by its parents, it may not touch land again until it breeds for the first time when it is five or six years old.

CHICKS AFLOAT

Typically, when a loon family has two chicks, the one that hatches first is often already larger and stronger by the time its sibling hatches, even when the hatching interval is less than a day. Graduate student Gary Dulin studied sibling rivalry among common loon chicks in Minnesota. He hid inside a floating blind that was shaped like a muskrat house with observation holes in it. Dulin observed that first-hatched chicks typically attained dominance over their sibling within four days of hatching, after pecking bouts that occurred three to four times a day. In these mini-battles, the agitated chicks would face off and stab or grasp each other's head and neck. Sometimes, the fights would start when the chicks were riding on a parent's back, and in the tussle, the two would tumble off while still holding onto each other until one chick finally submitted. The defeated chick would signal its submissiveness by lying flat on the water surface with its head and neck outstretched. If the dominant chick was not satisfied by this cowering gesture, it would peck its sibling repeatedly, sometimes forcing its head underwater. Eventually, even a simple stare could intimidate the weaker sibling, compelling it to back off and stay away. Once the dominance hierarchy was established, it was maintained throughout the summer.

The chicks in all loon species establish a similar dominance hierarchy. In red-throated loons, for example, three-quarters of the fights between siblings occurred in the first three days. A dominant chick might peck its sibling repeatedly to establish its position. The pecking order ensures that the dominant chick receives most of the feedings, and the younger red-throated chick often starves within a week of hatching. It's a similar story in Pacific loon chicks. They may fight for five days before a definitive winner emerges, but in some cases, the subordinate chick may accept defeat after just two days of conflict. When hand-raised Pacific loon chicks, less than six days old, were brought together in an enclosed area, they fought immediately and did not stop fighting until both combatants were so drenched that their swimming was impaired.

In Dulin's study of common loons, dominant chicks received up to 50 percent more food items than subordinate chicks, and three-quarters of the subordinate chicks perished within a month and a half of hatching. The parent loons showed no favouritism in feeding their chicks and simply responded to the most demanding chick. In British Columbia, I witnessed this early sibling interaction between two common loon chicks. When I first saw the chicks, the smaller of the two was floating with its face in the water. I thought it was dying until it suddenly lifted its head, only to drop it down again when its sibling approached. When one of the parents delivered a dragonfly nymph to the pair, the smaller chick conspicuously turned away as if uninterested, and the larger chick quickly grabbed the food. In Dulin's study, the speed with which a subordinate chick died was dependent on the quality and abundance of the feedings the chicks received, and how attentive their parents were.

Since so many loon chicks perish in the early days after hatching, why do females continue to lay two eggs? Biologists suggest several reasons for this. First, laying a second egg imposes a minimal energetic cost on the female. Second, the first egg may be sterile or defective, and laying a second one is insurance against such a situation. And finally, laying two eggs allows the parents to maximize the number of chicks they can raise when the family food supply is variable and unpredictable. By staggering the hatching of their two eggs, loons are able to adjust their brood size to a fluctuating food situation. There is nothing inherently wrong with the younger loon chick that perishes. It simply faces intense competition from its older sibling. When food is abundant, the dominant chick exerts less competition on its younger sibling, and the formerly doomed loon chick will grow normally and survive. Many other bird groups practise similar asynchronous hatching: penguins, boobies, cormorants, gulls, herons, storks, hawks, and owls. All do it for the same reason as loons—to adjust their brood size to a seasonally variable food supply.

In the early weeks after hatching, at least one parent is always closely shepherding the chicks. In Pacific loons, for example, during the first eighteen days of a chick's life, one of its parents is with it 98 percent of the time. When both parents are present, a chick may zigzag back and forth between them. As in all aspects of loon behaviour, the attentiveness of a parent is highly variable, and one sex or the other is not always more

devoted. It may reflect the strength and/or the longevity of the pair bond, or the age of the parents. The reason is unknown.

In common loon pairs that nest in partial-lake territories where there may be resident neighbours on either side of them, the adults initially move their newly hatched young to a so-called *nursery area*. The nursery area is generally a small protected cove or bay within the centre of the family's territory, sometimes encompassing a mere 15 percent of the total territory. The area is far enough from the nearest neighbour's territorial line that a chick won't accidentally trespass, be attacked, or possibly be killed. Typically, the selected sanctuary is sheltered from dangerous wind and wave action that might cause a chick to be accidentally separated from its parents. As well, the nurseries are usually in shallow water, often less than 1.5 metres (4.9 ft.) deep, with ample underwater vegetation, where there is an abundance of chick food in the form of aquatic invertebrates and small fish. As well as protection from storms and irascible neighbours, nurseries provide the hatchling loons with valuable foraging education—an ideal training ground for novice chicks with limited diving and prey-capturing ability. Families occupying whole-lake territories, as opposed

to partial-lake territories, may not sequester their chicks in a specific nursery area. Rather, they may wander throughout their entire territory, utilizing an array of protected, shallow, shoreline areas.

A loon chick becomes an accomplished diver weeks before it finally learns to fly. In the first day or two after hatching, a common loon chick dives about as well as a ping pong ball, bobbing helplessly at the surface. Give it a day or two more, and it can swim underwater the length of a bathtub, although it tires out quickly. I have watched these tiny fluffballs dive almost a metre (3.3 ft.) deep, desperately flailing their tiny stubby wings and paddling their miniature webbed feet to stay underwater. At

^ *Above.* A typical nursery area is a calm, shallow refuge where a loon hatchling is sheltered from dangerous wind, waves, and neighbours, and where abundant food is available for the parents to feed their chicks.

< *Opposite.* When this parent delivered a dragonfly nymph to its hatchlings, the subordinate chick, knowing its position in the dominance hierarchy, made no effort to intercept the food delivery.

two weeks of age, a chick's stamina has greatly improved, and if needed, it can swim underwater the length of a football field. By the time it is eight weeks old, its feet and legs are almost adult size, and it's a proficient diver, able to secure up to half its own food, even though it's still several weeks away from its maiden flight. The other loon species become skilled divers just as quickly. At one week of age, a hatchling red-throated loon can already stay underwater for twelve seconds and swim five metres (16 ft.).

Although hatchling loons quickly learn to dive, their hunting skills take much longer to develop, and for many weeks they are totally dependent on their parents to feed them. At two months of age, a common loon chick may still get half of its meals from its parents. When a loon chick is hungry, it peeps repeatedly and pecks and taps on the sides of its parent's beak and neck. When the chicks are very small, only one adult feeds the youngsters while the other parent remains nearby to watch over the vulnerable hatchlings. As the chicks get older, both adults may disappear underwater, foraging for deliverable meals, while the chicks float quietly on the surface, periodically peering underwater to watch for their parents.

Initially, almost all loon parents feed invertebrates to their hatchlings. Common meals include dragonfly and damselfly nymphs, diving beetles, caddisfly larvae, freshwater snails, and leeches. The loonlings quickly graduate to tiny fish, but the small width of a chick's gape limits the size of fish that it can swallow. The most manageable fish have a small head, a long slender body, and soft scales with no protective spines. I watched a week-old common loon chick reject a 7.5-centimetre (3 in.) rainbow trout that was repeatedly offered to it. Eventually, the thwarted mother swallowed the fish herself. Moments afterwards, the chick's father offered it a fingerling trout half the size of the rejected one, and the hungry youngster successfully managed to gulp it down.

Adult loons never regurgitate food to their young as their close relatives the penguins and albatrosses do. They simply present prey, one item at a time, held crosswise in their beak. If a chick is not hungry, or hesitates to accept a meal, the adult may splash the food around several times to perhaps stimulate the chick's feeding instinct. In one instance, an adult common loon waved a small fish back and forth close to its chick's head for almost twenty minutes, repeatedly dipping it in the water, before the reluctant youngster finally accepted the meal.

> *Opposite Top.* Freshwater leeches have almost the same nutritional value as a fish of a similar size. There were no fish in this lake, and the parents successfully fledged two chicks on a diet composed solely of leeches and other invertebrates.

Opposite Bottom. This common loon had caught a small rainbow trout that was too large for its chicks to swallow, so it eventually ate the fish itself.

For at least the first week of its life, a newly hatched loon chick is unable to maintain its body temperature, especially when it's paddling on the surface of a cold lake, where it can lose vital body heat through its featherless legs and feet. One drizzly late June morning in Alberta, the temperature was a chilly 7°C (45°F), and an adult common loon with two chicks was swimming offshore. The water temperature was certainly no warmer than the air that day, and both of the six-day-old chicks were riding on their parent's back. Back-riding is a frequent behaviour in the newly hatched chicks of common and yellow-billed loons, although it is infrequent in Arctic and Pacific loons, and rarely if ever seen in red-throated loons. Student researcher Tammy Black spent 167 hours watching a common loon pair with a single chick. In the first week of life, the young hatchling spent as much as two-thirds of its time riding on a parent's back. In week two, it spent less than a third of its time atop a floating adult, and by three weeks of age, it rarely hitched a ride. When there are two chicks in a family, both young may huddle together on the same parent or ride separately, each on a different parent.

Back-riding confers a number of advantages to young loon chicks. It's a feathery refuge where a tired, downy chick can

warm itself and be shielded from chilling winds, cold rains, and underwater predators, such as snapping turtles, largemouth bass, muskellunge, and northern pike. In Hanson Lake, Saskatchewan, in the 1970s, loon chicks were frequently found in the stomachs of northern pike at commercial fish plants. Loon parents constantly peer underwater watching for such predators, and a small chick is safest when it is riding on an adult's back. Aerial predators, such as bald eagles and large gulls, also pose a threat to small loon chicks that stray from an adult. When a chick is back-riding or floating beside a parent, the adult can usually defend it from an aerial predator. In northern Nunavut, I watched a pair of red-throated loons successfully defend their solitary downy chick from a pair of parasitic jaegers. The adults positioned themselves on either side of the chick. The predatory jaegers swooped down on the chick six or seven times, but each time, the adults pointed their sharp bills skyward and aggressively lunged at their attackers. The risk of injury was high for the jaegers, and they prudently abandoned the attack and flew away. Not every predator escapes unscathed. In the summer of 2019, a game warden in Maine found a dead bald eagle with a dead loon chick floating nearby. Initially, the warden thought the eagle had been shot, but a necropsy revealed that the

bird had been stabbed through the heart by the dagger-shaped beak of an adult loon, presumably the parent of the dead chick.

A chick will signal that it wants to back-ride by pecking at its parent's wing. The adult will usually lift its wing, allowing the youngster to scramble underneath and climb onto its back. If there are two chicks in the family, one may climb aboard while the other simply swims alongside the adult with its parent's wing covering it. Sometimes, an adult will sink in the water to allow a chick to mount from the rear, but I have seen this much less often than the lifted-wing approach. When the parent wants to jettison the chicks, it can simply dive and leave them bobbing on the surface or rise up and flap its wings, which causes the young to tumble off. When chicks want to dismount, I've seen them slide forward over the adult's shoulder, slip off the back, or leap over the parent's closed wing.

Loon chicks are not the only vulnerable young that ride on their parents' backs. The behaviour is common in grebes, South American sheldgeese, three species of swans, and seven species of ducks, including mergansers and common eiders. None of these chicks, including those of the common loon, ever rides when the adults are diving or flying.

> *Opposite.* Common loon chicks frequently ride on their parents' backs in the first two weeks of life but rarely do so after three weeks. The antics of these hatchlings are a delight to observe.

Perhaps the greatest threat to a young, downy chick's survival is not hypothermia, predatory fish, or taloned eagles but hostile adults of its own species that may kill chicks in their attempt to take over an occupied territory. Recall that intruders often fly over a territory on reconnaissance flights, and seeing chicks greatly increases a territory's desirability for takeover, so much so that intrusions increase by 60 percent when a territory produced young the previous year. Parent loons seem acutely aware of the threat posed by a trespassing adult, so when an intruder lands, one of the pair typically makes a long-distance dive and surfaces far away from its mate and chicks and tremolos, presumably hoping to distract the invader. Researchers Gabriella Jukkala and Walter Piper used a decoy to evaluate the response of common loon parents with chicks when an intruder appeared in their territory. Parents with vulnerable chicks less than two weeks old yodelled and penguin displayed more than parents with older chicks that had the ability to dive and escape underwater. The researchers also observed that males with two-chick broods yodelled almost three times more than males with single chicks. They concluded that parent loons defend chicks according to both their value and vulnerability.

When parent loons are forced to interact with intruders, the hatchlings will usually escape underwater to the nearest shoreline where they can hide. Biologist Rolph Davis, studying red-throated loons nesting along the western coast of Hudson Bay, observed how escaping chicks would swim along the lake bottom and stir up mud with their feet and then hide themselves in the murky water, constantly stirring up more sediment until they finally managed to escape to shore, where they could hide under an overhanging bank or in aquatic vegetation. Davis tried thirty-five times to catch chicks, and they eluded him every time using this murky-water strategy.

ADOPTION

Adoption in the natural world is uncommon. After all, all reproductive behaviours evolved to perpetuate the genes of the reproducing individuals. Adopting another's offspring and caring for them, unless those offspring are close relatives, does not help with this goal. In some cases, adopting an unrelated individual may reward a naïve adult with parenting experience that might later be beneficial in raising its own young. In other cases, however, the parents may simply not recognize their own young. In loons, any small hatchling within the confines of the parents' territory that vaguely resembles their natural offspring may be adopted without question. In essence, their behavioural wires get crossed.

In New Hampshire, in 2014, there were two examples of a displaced common loon chick being adopted by a neighbouring pair that already had their own two-chick brood. Both original broods were about one week old when their parents adopted the orphan chick, which was a similar age. Normally, chicks do not stray far from their parents, and neighbouring nursery areas are generally widely separated, so over the long course of evolution, there would be little need for adults to acquire strong chick identification cues.

It is one thing to adopt an orphan of the same species and quite another to take on the parenting of a completely different kind of bird. In 1978, graduate student Kenneth Abraham, working in Alaska, was shocked to see a brood of five spectacled eider ducklings swimming behind a mated pair of Pacific loons. Two weeks earlier, the loons and the eiders had been nesting ten metres (33 ft.) apart on the same small islet. When Abraham checked on the nests, the loon pair was accompanied by the ducklings; there were no loon chicks in sight and no adult female eider. The ducklings fed themselves on invertebrates and vegetation they gleaned from the water surface, and they periodically went ashore to rest and preen while the adult loons hid in emergent vegetation less than twenty metres (66 ft.) away. On several occasions, when the ducklings were less than two weeks old, the adult loons gave them food, and twice carried a single duckling on their backs. Once, when a predatory glaucous gull flew overhead, the adult loons immediately sounded the alarm with growling calls. The tiny eiders reacted by clumping tightly together and following the adults into the protection of some emergent vegetation. Abraham convincingly concluded that the adoption was

successful only because the ducklings appeared at a stage of the nesting cycle when the loons were hormonally receptive to the stimulus of young.

More recently, in 2016, photographer Doug Giles captured endearing images of a common loon in British Columbia with a common goldeneye duckling riding on its back. Giles told me that the adopted duckling stayed with the loons for almost a month, by which time it was nearly able to fly. He told me that when it would ride on the loons' backs, it was so heavy it would almost submerge the adult loon.

Another surprise adoption occurred in Wisconsin in 2019 when a common loon pair was seen with a mallard duckling resting on their backs, even when the orphan was already half their size. The parents were seen occasionally feeding fish to the duckling, even though the duck's usual diet is one of seeds, water plants, and invertebrates. The young mallard readily accepted small fish but rejected larger ones. A question arose. Having had such an atypical upbringing, when the duckling grew up, would it think of itself as a loon or a duck? Loon expert Walter Piper thought the duck might encounter some bumps along the way when it matured and sought a mate. He noted that crucial imprinting determines what a bird views as its parents and what its mate should look like. He joked, "It would be very surprising if this duck were to form a notion that a loon was a suitable mate, but your guess is as good as mine."

FEEDING THE FAMILY

As described earlier, many loon chicks are fed invertebrates in the early days after hatching, but such meagre fare is not the usual diet of most young loons, which are fed fish to fuel their rapid growth. In the Arctic, many nesting lakes are shallow, less than 1.5 metres (4.9 ft.) deep, and freeze to the bottom in winter. As a result, they're devoid of fish. In this situation, one solution for parent loons with hungry chicks is to take their young family on a road trip and walk to a deeper lake. Chicks are more agile on land than adults, so the youngsters usually make these terrestrial journeys by themselves, often with the vocal encouragement of their parents. In red-throated loons, for example, an overland move may start with the adults calling from a neighbouring pond. On Bathurst Island, in Canada's High Arctic, graduate student Christine Eberl recorded ten pairs of red-throats relocating to larger ponds. Most relocations

occurred when the nesting ponds began to freeze prematurely and the adults and their six-to-eight-week-old chicks found themselves confined to small openings. One overland journey was a remarkable one kilometre (0.6 mi.) in length, although most were less than fifty metres (164 ft.). Chicks are extremely vulnerable on land because of their limited mobility. In one instance, a four-week-old red-throated loon chick took 3.4 hours to scramble over 400 metres (437 yd.) of tundra. Moving to another pond is a risky endeavour and is likely never attempted unless unavoidable.

Pacific and Arctic loons also occasionally move their young overland from one pond to another. Most often, the move is less than 150 metres (164 yd.), and the chicks are usually older than two weeks of age. The evidence suggests that the moves occur

⌃ *Above.* This adult male common loon caught an unusually large rainbow trout that was too big for the young chick to swallow.

⟨ *Opposite.* In British Columbia, this common loon adopted a common goldeneye duckling. The orphan stayed with its adoptive parents for almost a month until it was nearly able to fly. Several times, the loons fed dragonfly nymphs to their adopted hatchling.

primarily when the energy demands of the growing chicks exceed the food available in the nest pond. New Hampshire biologist Harry Vogel has heard of several instances of this behaviour in common loons.

Loon parents feed their growing chicks whichever fish are easily captured and readily available. Among common loons, members of the perch family are a favourite because of their relatively easy catchability, but the parents never transport fish from one lake to another to feed their chicks. It's a different story for some of the other loon species. When foraging is poor in their nesting lake, Pacific, Arctic, and red-throated loon parents may fly to the ocean or to a larger nearby lake to fish for their young and carry prey back to them. For red-throated loons, such overland foraging flights are in fact the most common way they provision their young because so many red-throats nest in shallow, fishless lakes. Ocean foraging red-throated loons catch herring, capelin, Arctic char, grayling, sand lance, and sculpins to transport back to their chicks. Although the adults may forage up to twenty kilometres (12.4 mi.) from their nest pond, researcher Thomas Reimchen, studying red-throats in British Columbia's Haida Gwaii (formerly the Queen Charlotte Islands), reported that pairs generally foraged in the ocean just three kilometres (1.9 mi.) away, returning anywhere from eleven minutes to eight hours later, although their average return trip took less than an hour. Typically, the pairs made eleven foraging trips a day, and each time they returned with a single fish, positioned crosswise in their bills. As their chicks got older, the parents made fewer trips but delivered larger fish. There was a limit, however, on how large a fish an adult red-throat could transport. A chick would refuse a fish if it were too wide to swallow, although its length was never a problem. The adult red-throats had another constraint when it came to the size of fish they could transport. Like all loon species, red-throats have a very high wing loading, so carrying too large a fish could throw off the bird's aerodynamics, making flight impossible.

By the time most young loons are midway through the chick-rearing period, they are diving and foraging for their own meals, although their parents usually continue to feed them until they finally fledge at the end of summer. Until then, persistent begging for food continues. Chicks beg by swimming semicircles around their parent's breast and nibbling at the adult's neck and head feathers, chirping incessantly. In one

‹ *Opposite.* Red-throated loons typically forage for their chicks at sea or on large lakes near the nest pond and transport the meals to their young one fish at a time.

^ *Above.* This eight-week-old common loon chick was being raised on invertebrates on a fishless lake. The youngster was uncharacteristically aggressive toward its parents whenever they surfaced without any food. Such forcefulness is unusual.

instance, a large, hungry common loon chick begged for over an hour and a half while the parent pretended to sleep, continually steering away from the annoying youngster. The record for parental patience, however, must surely be held by an adult red-throated loon that had a hungry, chirping chick nibble at its breast feathers nonstop for two and a half hours.

Initially, chicks are clumsy at handling prey. Sometimes when an adult gives them a fish, they may drop it, and the parent has to retrieve it. It has been reported that parent loons first paralyze the fish by compressing it behind its gill covers, which makes it easier for the inexperienced young to cope with. I asked Dr. Michael Sullivan, an Alberta fisheries scientist, if this sounded plausible to him. He wrote back to me: "Interesting. There is no neurological reason for paralysis if a fish is compressed at that body location. The spinal cord

is well-protected from compression by the bony skull and strong backbone. The heart is usually close to the operculum [gill cover], but would be well-protected in most species from compression by the pectoral girdle." He suggested that anglers sometimes hold a fish upside down to "paralyze" it, but that only works occasionally. He had seen fish struggling violently in loons' beaks, and also seen them lying stiff and still. He could not explain the difference.

One of the common loon nesting lakes I have monitored for over ten years in Alberta has no fish in it, and the chicks are reared solely on invertebrates. I have never seen a parent loon transport a fish back from another lake, even though I suspect they regularly fly to them to fish for themselves. In the summer of 2021, the two eight-week-old chicks in that year's family seemed especially aggressive towards their parents and would

sometimes bite them on the neck when the adults surfaced after a dive without any prey to give them. The adults appeared to be well aware of the danger the chicks' large beaks posed to their eyes, and they would quickly turn away or dive to avoid the persistent harassment. In previous years, I had not seen the chicks in this lake be so forceful, and I wondered if a scarcity of food was making them desperate. Fortunately, both chicks fledged and likely flew to a nearby lake where the foraging was better. I'm guessing I'll never know why the young loons behaved as aggressively that summer as they did.

NASTY NEIGHBOURS

With such a title as "Nasty Neighbours," you might logically conclude that this section of the book delves into the many predators that loons must contend with, but in fact, I want to focus on what bad neighbours loons themselves can be, and how they terrorize others. At the beginning of Chapter 2, I recounted the story of how a male common loon inexplicably attacked and killed an unsuspecting American coot that was minding its own business and simply swimming along the shoreline about 200 metres (219 yd.) from the loon's nest. When I searched the scientific literature to find answers that would explain this murderous act, I was surprised to learn that this behaviour was not an infrequent event.

It turns out that loons regularly chase and harass neighbouring waterfowl during the nesting season. There are many records of common loons stalking and rushing American black ducks, wood ducks, ring-necked ducks, and common mergansers. This territorial intolerance is not restricted to common loons. In northern Ellesmere Island, I

❮ *Top Left.* At the northern tip of Ellesmere Island, Nunavut, at latitude 81° north, I watched this nesting red-throated loon chase a mother long-tailed duck and her four ducklings, forcing them to escape ashore.

Bottom Left. An aggressive Pacific loon, as in all loon species, adopts a hunched posture.

personally witnessed a red-throated loon chase a family of long-tailed ducks, forcing them to flee to shore. Others report Pacific loons chasing long-tailed and eider ducklings. As was the case in the killing of the hapless American coot, the aggressive loons often do not limit their interactions to simple pursuit and harassment. Multiple reports by Mark Sperry while studying common loons in Minnesota attest to this. In one case, a loon pair attacked a mother common goldeneye and her brood of seven one-week-old ducklings. When the ducklings scattered, one of the attacking loons caught a chick, killed it, and flung it aside; it then killed a second one before the duck family had a chance to safely escape to a floating mat of sedges. A year later, in the same lake, a pair of loons, possibly the same ones as before, attacked and killed four of the six ducklings of another female goldeneye. In both years, the ducklings died from lethal internal injuries or fatal punctures. The impact of loons on duckling survival can be substantial. In the same Minnesota lake, the number of goldeneye ducklings that were able to successfully fledge declined from an average of fourteen per year to only seven per year once loons began nesting on the lake.

Elsewhere, in Canada's Northwest Territories, a pugnacious common loon attacked and killed a young red-breasted merganser just days before it would have fledged. In the week that followed, five other ducklings from the same brood mysteriously disappeared. The researcher who reported the original killing suspected that the loon may have been responsible.

Common loons don't only kill defenceless ducklings—they attack adult ducks as well. In northern British Columbia, a male loon attacked and grabbed an adult female redhead duck. With the duck still in its bill, the loon rose vertically in the water in a dramatic penguin display and violently shook the helpless victim from side to side. The redhead was still alive when the loon released it but died minutes later from a hemorrhaging tear of its liver.

Common loons are not the only waterfowl killers; Pacific loons can be just as murderous. In Prudhoe Bay, Alaska, a Pacific loon made a cagey underwater attack on a three-week-old snow goose gosling. After sustaining eight to ten strikes from the aggressive loon, the gosling managed to struggle ashore but died twelve hours later. Elsewhere, in the Yukon Flats of Interior Alaska, a Pacific loon attacked and killed a four-day-old lesser

^ *Above*. In Canada's High Arctic, a summer aggregation of six Pacific loons indulged in a textbook sequence of loon social interactions, including circle swimming, bill-dipping, surface rushing, wing-rowing, and penguin displays.

scaup duckling by grabbing it and shaking it forcefully. The mother duck briefly tried to defend her offspring, then quickly escaped with the remainder of her brood. As a general rule, loons are a much greater threat to waterfowl on small nesting lakes, where the likelihood of encounters is high.

Loons generally attack their victims in one of two ways. They either swim on the surface with their neck outstretched low over the water and stab or grab, or they approach underwater and explosively surface under the unsuspecting victim, once again using their dagger-shaped bill to grab or stab.

When I first shared my photos of the coot-killing loon, many of the recipients were surprised and shocked by the ferocity of the attack and admitted it drastically changed their opinion of loons. So why does this seemingly beautiful, peaceful symbol of the wilderness so frequently chase and harass—

and sometimes kill—its waterfowl neighbours? Biologists Ian Kirkham and Stephen Johnson proposed four possible explanations. First, the attack could be a predatory attempt, but most loon victims are not eaten by their attackers, with the one exception of a common loon that caught and ate a common eider duckling. Another possibility is that the attacking loon is simply defending its nesting lake from waterfowl that could compete with it for a limited food supply. Unfortunately, the diets of most ducks and geese that loons harass don't overlap at all with that of the loons. The two exceptions to this are the common and red-breasted mergansers, both of which eat fish.

Could it also be that killer male loons are "showing off" to their female partners, and their aggressive displays towards waterfowl are intended to convince their mates of their ability to defend the family territory? The problem with this explanation

162

is that males may not always be the ones doing the killing, and when they are, their female partners are often not present to witness their machismo. The fourth, and most plausible, explanation for the aggression shown towards waterfowl is that the behaviour is actually aberrant and nonadaptive. Biologist Gregory Robertson suggests that perhaps loons can't differentiate between the threat of non-loon young and other loon chicks and therefore respond with aggression. Killing young waterfowl may have evolved in the context of killing competing young loons, which is known to occur regularly after a hostile takeover. The culprits may simply be genetically programmed to reflexively attack any small moving foreign young in their nesting territory. Even if this explains the murder of young waterfowl, it doesn't explain why loons sometimes kill adult waterfowl as well.

SUMMER SOCIALS

On July 18, 2021, I was on Victoria Island, Nunavut, watching a pair of Pacific loons incubate their single egg when suddenly four loons landed on their nesting lake. The incubating bird and its mate joined the group, and all six began to socialize, running through a textbook sequence of loon displays: circle swimming, head turning, wing flapping, and quick shallow dives. Within a minute, the real excitement started with splash dives, multiple surface rushes, one bird chasing another, and different birds engaged in energetic penguin displays. I was so thrilled by the photo action that I don't recall hearing any vocalizations. Usually, such vigorous social behaviour is accompanied by vociferous yelps, wails, and tremolos. After fourteen minutes, the four outsiders abruptly flew away, leaving the resident pair to continue incubating their egg.

Ten years earlier, in July, I was on a lake in central British Columbia observing a single pair of nesting common loons. An hour after sunrise, fourteen birds landed, while five others flew overhead but didn't land. The birds gathered in the centre of the lake and swam in unison, shallow diving and bill-dipping, and making a few surface rushes and a single penguin display. The group slowly splintered apart, and gradually they all departed. The gathering lasted about an hour and a half.

Veteran loon researcher Judith McIntyre called these temporary summer get-togethers *social gatherings*. Most often, these social gatherings occur in early morning or late afternoon and last from a few minutes to several hours. In one study of common loons in Michigan and Wisconsin, gatherings lasted an average of nineteen minutes in July versus thirty-one minutes in August. In the beginning, the groups typically number three or four birds, but as the breeding season winds down, the numbers increase and may swell to more than twenty participating loons. In addition to the territorial residents on whose lake the gatherings occur, the participants might include unpaired birds, failed breeders, birds evicted from their territories, and even successful breeders. The birds often aggregate in neutral waters, perhaps to signal peaceful intentions, and as the season progresses, the displays and behaviours become less aggressive, conceivably a consequence of declining sex hormones.

The purpose of these social gatherings is still unclear but may serve several functions, including familiarity with neighbours, reconnaissance of potential territories, and practice with flocking behaviour in advance of autumn migration. Biologists know more about social gatherings in common loons, but the other loon species also form similar transient groupings in midsummer, and likely for the same reasons.

FLIGHT SCHOOL GRADUATION

In the early days of the COVID-19 pandemic, before I was vaccinated, the silver lining in those many months of isolation and social distancing was the chance to once again spend many hours in the out of doors, intensively following the lives of three families of common loons near my home in Calgary, Alberta. Because I was with the loons so much, I witnessed crucial moments in their lives, and one of those memorable events was graduation from flight school.

> *Opposite.* After several days of aborted takeoff attempts, this eleven-week-old common loon chick finally became airborne and left its natal lake on its maiden flight. Once a young loon can fly, it may loiter on its natal lake for several weeks before it finally leaves.

On September 3, 2020, the sole surviving chick on one of the three lakes I was monitoring was already practising his flying skills when I arrived at 8:25 a.m. Three different times, he flapped and ran across the water for a distance of twenty to thirty metres (22–33 yd.), exercising his flight muscles. On the fourth exercise session, he flapped across the whole length of the lake and actually lifted off momentarily before crash landing into the water just as he was about to plough into the shoreline. The aborted flight attempt came moments after his parent had taken off. I suspected that the adult's departure stimulated the chick to follow. The adult circled the lake twice and from high overhead repeatedly gave tremolo calls. In response, the chick called with a juvenile version of a yodel, even adopting the low stretch posture used when a yodel is given by an adult territorial male. After one or two minutes, the adult flying overhead banked in a steep glide and landed with a splash, rejoining the chick.

When I returned early the next morning, the unexpected happened at 9:20 a.m. The parent and chick swam to the far end of the lake. When both birds stretched their necks upwards in an alert posture, I felt something exciting was about to happen.

^ *Above.* A young common loon chick, like all young loons, goes through three different plumages during its development from hatchling to a fledged juvenile. Pictured here (*left to right*) are two one-week-old chicks, a three-week-old chick, a seven-week-old chick, and an eleven-week-old chick.

Seconds later, the adult took off, followed almost immediately by the chick. I was certain the chick's takeoff was wishful thinking on its part and that it would simply flap and splash as it had done the previous day. Suddenly, the young loon was aloft and passing a mere three metres (9.8 ft.) above my head. It seemed to have trouble gaining altitude to clear the trees, and it circled the lake three times before it was finally above the treetops. With that achieved, it was gone. I hung around for a couple of hours, but the loons never returned. The lake was one that had no fish in it, and it's likely the chick moved to one that did, either by following his parent or finding one by chance.

For a loon chick to fly, it needs the right feathers, which take time to grow. As mentioned earlier, all newly hatched loon chicks go through two downy feather phases, the first being gradually replaced by the second when the chicks are two to three weeks old. Juvenile contour feathers are more waterproof than down, and these first appear on the young loon's underside when it's about one month old. In the month following that, grey contour feathers spread over the rest of the bird's body, while a few remaining tufts of baby fuzz cling to the young loon's head and neck. Flight feathers are the last to appear, and by ten weeks of age, the chick is fully feathered for flight. All it needs after that is one or two more weeks of exercise and practice, and it's up, up, and away. Most common loon chicks finally begin flying when they are eleven to thirteen weeks old. This nice, tidy sequence of feather events leading to flight applies to common and yellow-billed loons. The sequence is somewhat shorter in the smaller loon species, with Arctic and Pacific loon chicks fledging after eight to nine weeks and young red-throated loons as soon as six to seven weeks.

Loon parents will continue to feed their chicks as long as they remain in the family territory, but in most cases, the adults abandon the nesting lake ahead of the chicks, with each adult leaving separately. Young loons may loiter on the nesting lake for a week or two, feeding themselves. The availability of food probably influences when both the adults and chicks eventually leave. Young red-throated loons depart more quickly from their nesting lake, frequently within less than four days of their first flight. After their maiden flight to the ocean, young red-throats may continue to be fed by one or both parents for a week or so, something that no other species of loon has been seen to do.

For a loon chick to reach fledging age is rarely a certainty; in fact, the majority never make it. To begin with, many eggs never hatch. Recall that in different studies of common loons, the egg hatching rates vary from 38 to 70 percent. In Pacific loons, the hatching rates swing between a dismal 28 percent and a hopeful 92 percent. Red-throated loon hatching rates also vary greatly, ranging from a high of 78 percent down to a low of 33 percent. Even when an egg hatches successfully, the chick survival rate to fledging is never 100 percent. In common loons, it varies from 67 to 94 percent. In a study of Arctic loons in Finland, it averaged just 47 percent, whereas in a Scottish study, it varied between 57 and 67 percent. Red-throated loons appear to have the poorest success raising chicks, with a fledging rate sometimes as low as 38 percent. Predator pressure is one of the most important determinants of fledging success, but food availability and inclement weather are other important factors. The most vulnerable time for a loon chick is the initial two to three weeks after hatching. If a chick can survive those first weeks, it will likely make it to fledging.

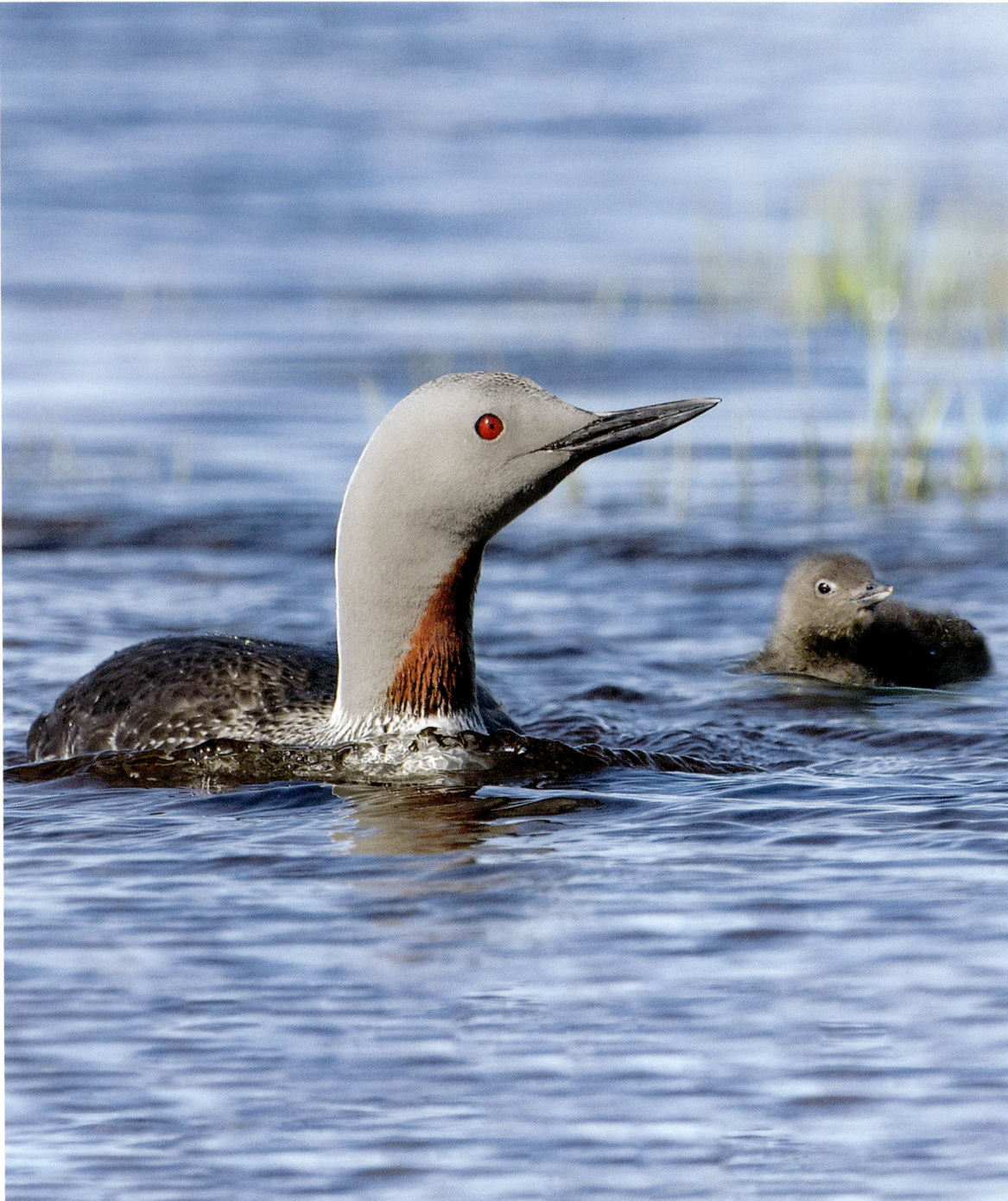

In the end, the survival of loons as a species, like all long-lived seabirds, depends on them enduring some years of breeding failure balanced by some years of success, with these being spread over a lengthy reproductive lifespan of a decade or two. If you combine the annual egg and chick losses of all the territorial loon pairs in a given area, you arrive at the average number of fledged young. Thus, for common loons, it ranges from 0.28 to 0.96 fledged chicks per pair per year. When it falls below 0.48, a population begins to decline. For red-throated loons, fledging success can vary between 0.17 and 1.0 fledged chicks per pair per year. And for Arctic loons in Scotland, the fledging success ranges from 0.23 to 0.29 chicks per pair per year. Biologists use this hodgepodge of numbers to monitor whether a loon population is growing, declining, or stable. The take-home message is a simple one. For all loon species, reproduction, influenced by a multitude of factors, varies dramatically from year to year, and from location to location, and the continued survival of every loon species is reliant on a long reproductive lifespan that can weather periodic failures.

CHAPTER 7
Oceanbound

I first went to Mexico's Baja California forty years ago. Then, I was a freshly minted freelancer hired as a combination zodiac driver, onboard naturalist, and ship's doctor on an ecotourism vessel that was cruising the lengthy coastline of the peninsula. Back then, in 1982, Cabo San Lucas, at the southern tip of the peninsula, was a sleepy little Mexican village. When I went ashore one night for a break from the ship, the only entertainment the staff and I could find was a rooster fight in a dingy local bar. It was a gruesome, sanguineous spectacle. Today, Cabo is one of Mexico's premier tourist destinations. The sacrificial roosters have been replaced by tens of thousands of sun-seeking tourists. Since 2015, I have been back to Baja California half a dozen times, but not for the tequila or the tourism at the cape— rather, to experience the beauty and natural wonder of the whale-rich waters of its coastal bays. A trio of lagoons indent the Pacific coastline of the peninsula and offer sheltered waters for mother grey whales giving birth to vulnerable calves. This is the biological magnet that lures me to Mexico each winter, but I derive an equal amount of joy from watching the migrant birds that share these waters with the whales. Two of the migrants are common and Pacific loons. Both of these diving seabirds frequent the lagoons, where there are abundant small fish. The Pacific loons also forage at the mouths of the lagoons, where strong tidal currents race through constricted channels. My Mexican naturalist friends tell me that no one has studied loons in these warm subtropical lagoons, so the biology of these wintering birds remains a tantalizing mystery.

AUTUMN GET-TOGETHERS

Up to this point in the review of the annual life of an adult loon, I've detailed two different occasions when it might join a temporary grouping. First, in early spring, some loons may gather on ice-free lakes or the open-water areas of the coastal pack ice waiting for their nesting lakes to melt. In these situations, the individuals interact very little, and they rarely vocalize. They behave a lot like subway commuters silently waiting on the platform for the next train. Later, in midsummer, a second type of transient grouping occurs when nonbreeders, failed breeders, and others intrude on occupied territories and interact with each other and the territory owners. In the process, the participants become familiar with their neighbours and acquire potentially valuable information on the quality of

< *Opposite.* In late summer, yellow-billed loons, like many other loons, may gather on large staging lakes to forage in preparation for migration.

the territory, its owners, and the prospects for a future hostile takeover. These summer gatherings, unlike the ones in spring, are filled with ritualized displays, noisy vocalizations, and lots of social interactions.

In late summer and early autumn, many loons aggregate in a third type of gathering, one that is a preamble to migration. In some situations, it may be tough to distinguish between summer social gatherings and these premigration get-togethers, and in fact, one may slowly transition into the other. By late summer, the sex hormones that are the principal drivers of aggression in loons have waned, and the birds can flock together agreeably. At this time of the year, observers may see dozens of yellow-billed loons clustered offshore from Alaska's Coastal Plain, hundreds of Pacific loons floating in Hudson Bay, or hundreds of common loons rafting in the large lakes of northern Saskatchewan. In North America, well-known autumn staging areas for common loons include Walker Lake in Nevada, Mille Lacs Lake in Minnesota, and Flathead Lake in Montana. The Great Lakes are another favourite premigration staging area where thousands of common and red-throated loons may temporarily aggregate.

The two things that all of these early autumn staging areas seem to have in common are clear water and abundant small fish. During the day, the loons may split up into smaller groups of a dozen or two, but they move back together again at night, loosely clustering over deep water. The loons that gather in these staging waters are often unfamiliar with the local foraging conditions, and the schooling fish on which they often feed may be widely dispersed and hard to locate. By foraging in a group, the birds benefit by having many eyes searching for prey, and when it's located everyone profits.

In many cases, these premigration gatherings begin to disperse by the end of September, when the loons finally head south to their eventual wintering grounds. In the Arctic, where the breeding season is short and winters come fast and early, everything is accelerated, and some of these premigration gatherings may form as early as the end of July. This is in stark contrast to some of the most southern nesting common loons, where the juveniles may not abandon their staging lakes until much later. In the Adirondacks of New York State, for example, a satellite-tracked juvenile moved from lake to lake, starting on August 21 and loitered until December 4, apparently staying

> *Opposite*. Common loons in premigration gatherings hoot repeatedly to stay in contact with each other.

^ *Above.* When a common loon moults its breeding feathers and begins to acquire its winter plumage, the first whitish-grey feathers appear at the base of the bill, as if the bird is growing a tiny beard.

ahead of the annual autumn freeze until it eventually migrated to the coast. Adults from the same population of common loons flew directly to the coast in a nonstop flight lasting just five to six hours.

OUT WITH THE OLD, IN WITH THE NEW

Feathers, like hair and fingernails, are dead structures. Over time, they become brittle, faded, and frayed. Once they wear out, they need to be replaced. The process of routinely replacing a coat of feathers is called *moulting*. Loons, like many birds, have one set of feathers for the breeding season and another for the winter season. Moulting in birds is energetically expensive, sometimes requiring as much as ten to thirty times a species' daily energy costs. Consequently, the process may be prolonged in loons,

starting in late summer and extending well into winter. In general, a healthy loon with a nutritious diet moults faster than one that is unwell or has less food to eat. Typically, nonbreeding adults moult sooner than adults with young, who must additionally contend with the protracted stress of raising chicks.

The beautiful, distinctive plumage that loons flaunt during the breeding season is the one with which most people are familiar. In common loons, the replacement of these elegant feathers begins in August, often while they are still tending young. The black feathers at the base of the bill and on the chin are the first to be replaced by whitish-grey ones, which make the loon look like it is growing a small white beard. From there, the moult spreads over the lower head and down the neck. By late September, the plumage of certain adults may already look like that of juveniles. Many may acquire full winter plumage by the middle of October, although for most, it takes until early December for this to happen. As discussed, the timing of moulting in loons is highly variable.

One of the interesting aspects of moulting in loons is the delayed replacement of their flight feathers. Having replaced all of their body feathers in the autumn, loons wait until the middle of winter, typically between January and March, to grow their new flight feathers. Most seabirds replace their wing feathers one at a time in order not to be grounded. Loons lose theirs all at once and are flightless for two to three weeks while the new feathers grow in. Loons have such a high wing loading that they cannot afford to lose even one or two wing feathers without it having a major impact on their flying ability. Their solution is to moult in winter, when most are on the ocean where food is readily available and the need for flying minimal.

The adult moult in red-throated loons is slightly different than in the other four species. Rather than replace their flight feathers in winter, they moult during autumn migration when they find themselves in a safe staging area where they can loiter and be flightless for a time. They continue their migration once their moult is complete.

HEADING SOUTH—FROM FRESH WATER TO SALT

For the vast majority of loons, autumn is the season to migrate from their freshwater nesting lakes to the ocean where they will spend the winter. In recent years, however, a small number of common loons in North America, less than 5 percent of

^ *Above.* The red-throated loon, unlike the other four species, replaces its flight feathers in autumn while it is migrating to its wintering grounds.

the total, has wintered in freshwater lakes and reservoirs, primarily in the southwestern and southeastern regions of the United States. Notwithstanding this minor trend, there are good reasons why most loons spend the winter at sea. Temperate seas don't freeze, and moulting loons benefit from unrestricted mobility at a time when they are flightless and vulnerable. There is also a greater variety and abundance of food in the ocean than in most freshwater habitats, and twice each day, the incoming tide delivers naïve prey to a loon's feeding grounds.

In Chapter 3, the distribution maps for all five species of loons outline their nesting grounds in red and their wintering grounds in blue. When they can, loons typically migrate

between their summer and winter areas by following the coastlines on either side of the continents, and sometimes their routes seem unnecessarily lengthy and circuitous. For example, Pacific loons nesting on the Ungava Peninsula in northern Quebec initially migrate west to the Beaufort Sea, off the northern tip of the Yukon, and from there follow a coastal route, possibly ending as far south as Mexico's Baja California—a potential journey of more than 11,000 kilometres (6,835 mi.). These same Pacific loons could simply migrate east less than 2,500 kilometres (1,553 mi.) to the ice-free waters south of Newfoundland. Why they don't do that is still unknown.

Naturally, any of the multitude of loons that nests in the interior of a continent must by necessity travel overland, at least initially, to reach the ocean, and inland sightings are frequent. For example, in 2020, a yellow-billed loon was seen near Calgary, Alberta, and every year dozens of red-throated loons are sighted on the Ottawa River in Ontario.

The details of the southward autumn migration in loons are pretty much the same as was discussed in Chapter 5 for their spring migration north. Loons migrate during the day, and most make their way south in stages. Being heavy-bodied birds with relatively small wings, they can't afford to significantly pad their bodies in advance of migration with heavy layers of fat to sustain them on a lengthy flight. As a result, they usually land at the end of each day and often stay in one location for several days while they forage and prepare for the next stage of their travels. In general, the pace of autumn migration is more leisurely than in spring, as there is no pressure for the birds to establish breeding territories. Consequently, they may stop more often and loiter for longer periods.

Migrating loons fly alone, in twos and threes, or in small loose groups of up to a dozen or two, with individuals often separated by several hundred metres, or as far apart as one kilometre (0.6 mi.). In common loons, it is traditionally understood that failed breeders typically migrate before those with young, adults before juveniles, and females before males, but with the advent of satellite tagging, researchers are seeing a lot of variations to this pattern. As far as the other loon species are concerned, there is too little data to draw any conclusions.

When migrating over water, loons often fly low and fast. Along the coast of California, Pacific loons are seen in autumn flying at heights of less than ten metres (33 ft.)—sometimes just above the ocean surface. Loons fly at much higher altitudes when flying over land. Common loons, for example, routinely fly at altitudes of 1,500 to 2,700 metres (4,921–8,858 ft.) and are difficult to see without binoculars.

Stormy weather can sometimes be a danger to migrating loons. In heavy fog and rain, when landmarks are obscured, the birds usually stay grounded. If they happen to be flying when a severe rainstorm overtakes them, impairing visibility, they may mistakenly land on a rain-slick highway thinking it is the glassy surface of a lake. Loons can't take off from land, and they become stranded and usually perish unless some good Samaritans rescue them. One year, in mid-November near Joelton, Tennessee, an early winter storm fooled several dozen common loons into landing on local highways. Fortunately, the birds were discovered by some police officers and passersby, who took them to a rehabilitation centre where they were cared for until they could safely be released.

The satellite tracking of migratory loons began in 1998 when miniature transmitters, weighing just 47 grams (1.7 oz.)—the weight of two AA batteries—were surgically implanted under the skin of five adult common loons nesting in Wisconsin and

‹ *Opposite.* Migrating Pacific loons, like all loons, migrate singly or in small, uncoordinated groups of a dozen or less.

Michigan. Initially, all five loons moved to the Great Lakes, where three of them lingered for several weeks. From their stopover in the Great Lakes, each followed one of two migration routes, either eastward across the Appalachian Mountains to the coastal waters off North Carolina or Florida or straight southward on an overland path west of the Appalachians to the Gulf of Mexico. The total distances migrated ranged from 1,884 to 2,121 kilometres (1,171 to 1,318 mi.), with all of the migrants arriving on their wintering grounds by late November or early December, having taken weeks to reach their destination.

Several summers later, researcher Kevin Kenow and his colleagues captured seventeen adult common loons in New York, New Hampshire, and Maine and implanted satellite transmitters in them to see if loons that nested closer to the ocean had shorter migrations, and indeed they did. The adults from Maine and New Hampshire wintered along the coast of Maine only 150 to 239 kilometres (93–149 mi.) from their breeding lakes. Loons from New York migrated somewhat farther, wintering off the coasts of Rhode Island, Massachusetts, or New Jersey. The longest migration made by any of the seventeen loons being tracked was 527 kilometres (327 mi.). Any

of these distances could be managed by a healthy adult loon, flying at 100 kilometres per hour (62 miles per hour), in a single nonstop flight of just one and a half to five hours.

Researchers wondered if the weight of a common loon was influenced by the distance it migrated. To answer this question, biologist Carrie Gray and a dozen colleagues compared the body weights and the migration distances of loons from eleven states and seven provinces spread across the breadth of North America. The body weights of the sampled loons varied from 2.7 to 7.6 kilograms (5.9 to 16.8 lb.), and their migration distances likewise differed greatly, ranging from 154 to 4,700 kilometres (96 to 2,920 mi.). The results of the study were crystal clear. The common loons with the heaviest body weights, those from Maine and New Hampshire, migrated the shortest distances, whereas those from central Canada and the Upper Great Lakes, weighing the least, migrated the farthest. The researchers concluded that the most likely explanation for this relationship was related to the heavy wing loading in loons. The heavier the loon, the more energy it takes for it to take off and fly, and heavy body weights are only possible if the migration distance is short.

‹ *Opposite.* It's unclear how juvenile common loons learn where to spend the winter as they don't accompany their parents during migration.

Male loons are always larger than their female partners, but the difference between them varies. Gray discovered that the weight differences between male and female partners were affected by the pairs' migration distances. In short-distance migrants, which travelled less than 1,500 kilometres (932 mi.), the males weighed roughly 25 percent more than their female partners. This was in contrast to the medium-distance migrants, whose journeys ranged from 1,500 to 3,500 kilometres (932 to 2,175 mi.), in which the males weighed just 21 percent more than the females.

In recent years, the continued use of satellite tracking has led to some remarkable discoveries in the migration details of some of the other loon species. When a dozen yellow-billed loons were tracked from their nesting grounds on the northern coastal plains of Alaska, researchers were surprised to see them migrate along the Asian coastline as far south as the Yellow Sea in China—this was the first evidence of a trans-Pacific migration. Even more unexpected were the migration details of Alaskan red-throated loons. In a 2018 study, lead researcher Sarah McCloskey compared the migration distances and wintering destinations of four widely separated Alaskan populations of

nesting red-throated loons. The birds that McCloskey tracked were located in (from north to south) the Arctic Coastal Plain, the Seward Peninsula, the Yukon-Kuskokwim delta, and the Copper River delta. Loons from the three southern populations simply migrated to wintering grounds along the Pacific coast of North America. McCloskey described their movements as a *chain migration*, in which the more northerly nesting populations generally wintered in more northerly latitudes.

The migratory movements of red-throated loons from the Arctic Coastal Plain, the most northern of the four Alaskan study groups, yielded the biggest surprises. Some of them underwent the longest migrations ever recorded for a species of loon flying to its wintering grounds—an average distance of 7,993 kilometres (4,967 mi.), with the longest journey a remarkable 9,278 kilometres (5,765 mi.)! Most of these long-distance travellers flew westward to eastern Siberia, and from there, they journeyed along the Pacific coast of Russia's Kamchatka Peninsula and the Japanese archipelago, ending up off the tip of the Korean Peninsula.

Given that loons have a high wing loading, McCloskey expected that they would make frequent stopovers on

> *Opposite.* Yellow-billed loons that winter in East Asia face far greater exposure to contaminants due to the disposal of hazardous chemicals being less strictly controlled than those loons wintering along the Pacific coast of North America.

their lengthy journey, and indeed they did. The stopovers averaged forty-five days but ranged from twenty-six to sixty-two days. These important refuelling and resting locations often coincided with major coastal upwellings where marine productivity was high and food abundant.

WINTER VACATION

The first loon book I ever read was Tom Klein's *Loon Magic*, published in 1985. Near the end of the book, Klein makes an observation that I have never forgotten. He jokes, "Interest in wintering loons is somewhat like Christmas sales of air conditioners in Bangor [Maine]—a little restrained. It's no surprise. The striking summer bird of the north with the beautiful voice becomes a drab, shy coastal resident. The two things northerners love about loons—their dramatic plumage and haunting calls—are not enjoyed by southerners." I'm as guilty as anyone for focusing on loons when they are at their most vociferous and beautiful. I have literally tens of thousands of loon photographs taken on their summer nesting grounds but just a few dozen images when they are quietly vacationing on the ocean in winter.

Veteran loon researcher James Paruk and his colleagues knew that adult common loons were more than 80 percent faithful to their summer nesting grounds but wondered if they displayed the same fidelity to their wintering grounds. Once again, satellite tracking came to the rescue. Paruk was able to show that 85 percent of the time the loons he was tracking repeatedly returned to their same coastal wintering locations in California's Morro Bay, Louisiana's Barataria Bay, Maryland's Chincoteague Bay, and Massachusetts's Cape Cod. In Barataria Bay, for example, five of the loons he followed were found within a kilometre (0.6 mi.) of where they had been originally captured. Paruk suggested that many adults may actually overwinter in the same location throughout their life. The loons in his study wintered within a relatively small area of just ten to twenty square kilometres (6.2–12.4 sq. mi.). One reason for their limited movement may be a consequence of the midwinter flightless period they experience when they moult and replace all their wing feathers.

Where a loon chooses to winter is undoubtedly driven by the abundance and availability of fish and other prey, as well as the depth and clarity of the water. Most often, they stay within a few kilometres of shore in sheltered channels and protected bays and inlets, avoiding river mouths where the turbidity from suspended sediments reduces underwater visibility. In a study led by Kevin Kenow, half of the monitored common loons wintering off the northeast coast of the United States were within 1.3 kilometres (0.8 mi.) of the shoreline, and virtually all of them were within 10.5 kilometres (6.5 mi.). During winter gales, however, loons may temporarily move farther offshore to avoid the roiling surf.

Not all coastal areas are equally attractive to loons, and some attract great densities of wintering loons. For example, thousands of Eurasian-nesting red-throated loons overwinter

∧ *Above.* Four of the world's five species of loons may overwinter in the sheltered waters of coastal British Columbia; only the Arctic loon does not.

‹ *Opposite.* Red-throated loons, such as this one photographed in Canada's High Arctic, often abandon their nesting lakes in mid- to late-August, before they begin to moult their breeding plumage.

in the German Bight of the North Sea. A similar situation occurs off the coast of Kyushu in the Japanese archipelago, where thousands of Arctic and Pacific loons while away the winter. On the Pacific coast of North America, the highest densities of wintering common loons occur around Haida Gwaii, British Columbia, in Puget Sound, Washington, and in Monterey Bay, California. On the Atlantic side, where 70 percent of the continent's common loons overwinter, large numbers occur in the Gulf of Maine, off the coasts of Virginia and North Carolina, and along the northern edge of the Gulf of Mexico.

On their wintering grounds, loons spend roughly half their time foraging, which is about the same as on their breeding lakes. The remainder of their day is occupied with preening, loafing, swimming, and flying about. Astonishingly little time is spent interacting with other loons. In some cases, social interactions make up less than 1 percent of a loon's day.

In general, wintering loons forage alone and don't typically defend a feeding territory. However, when a large school of fish is located, several loons may forage close to each other at the same time. Such is the case with Pacific loons in Active Pass, British Columbia, where dozens of loons may be seen diving and feeding together on the schooling herring that seasonally aggregate in this area of upwelling and strong tidal currents. Although loons may forage collectively, there is no evidence that individuals actually coordinate their behaviour to benefit the participants. Penguins, a close relative of loons, often forage in groups, but it is still every bird for itself, with no coordination reported.

Common loons, like all loons, are visual hunters and relatively shallow divers. On their wintering grounds, the hefty birds typically forage in water just 1.5 to 5.5 metres (4.9–18 ft.) deep, and they make dives lasting up to ninety seconds. The dives of Pacific loons in a Monterey Bay study averaged seventy-seven seconds, and those of red-throated loons just forty-nine seconds. Between foraging bouts, common loons usually move farther from shore to loaf and preen in water 5.5 to 9 metres (18–30 ft.) deep. Although they usually forage alone during the day, the birds often clump together in loose rafts containing up to several dozen birds and spend the night floating collectively over deep water—a predator surveillance strategy.

Sometimes, a foraging loon may join a group of other hungry seabirds. In Active Pass, mentioned above, the Pacific loons sometimes join Bonaparte's gulls and Brandt's

> *Opposite.* During severe winter weather, when the turbidity of the water increases, common loons may switch from hunting fish to foraging for crabs and other crustaceans. Researchers suspect that the birds use their bill to probe the seabed to help them locate these bottom dwellers.

cormorants. Elsewhere, loons may form mixed feeding groups with rhinoceros auklets, scoters, western grebes, and western and glaucous-winged gulls. Such mixed groups usually form after gulls make an initial discovery of surface or near-surface schools of baitfish, such as sand lances, Pacific herring, smelts, and northern anchovies. These feeding groups are ephemeral, often ending in less than fifteen minutes when their prey escapes to deeper water. Throughout, the birds appear to tolerate each other with a minimum of interaction and antagonism.

Once a loon reaches adult size, it is a large, muscular bird armed with a dagger-like beak and a potentially aggressive temperament. Few predators are audacious enough to threaten it on its nesting grounds; however, in Wisconsin, there is an isolated record of a fisher (a large species of weasel) killing an incubating common loon. A bald eagle, also in Wisconsin, attacked an adult male common loon, landing on the bird's back and holding it underwater for a few moments before the loon successfully struggled free. When the loon was examined three weeks later, it was healthy with no visible signs of injury. Off the coast of Vancouver Island, a bald eagle made another predatory attack on a loon, but this time it was successful. The victim was a

juvenile Pacific loon, probably half the size of an adult common loon, which made it an easier target for the eagle than the bird in Wisconsin just described. The juvenile loon was all the more vulnerable because it was soiled with oil and massively infected with tapeworms, which may have weakened it.

In contrast to the relatively minor predatory threats facing loons on their nesting grounds, the dangers confronted on wintering grounds are a slightly different matter, as the potential predators are bigger and hungrier. In 1988, marine biologists Marianne Riedman and James Estes were surprised to discover that adult male sea otters in northern California were preying on seabirds. Normally, these fuzzy-faced carnivores feed on sea urchins, abalone, crabs, and clams. Among the seabird victims were wintering common loons, as well as western grebes, gulls, scoters, and cormorants. Recall that all of these birds regularly join mixed feeding groups with wintering loons, and they frequently share a common foraging ground with them. In the cases observed by Riedman and Estes, the otters grabbed the victims from underwater when the unsuspecting birds were floating on the surface. The authors noted that predation on seabirds was a relatively new

< *Opposite.* A juvenile common loon in its first winter on the ocean does not moult its flight feathers, as adults do, but waits until its first summer alone at sea, when it has access to abundant food to energetically fuel its feather replacement.

behaviour for sea otters, indicative of the carnivore's ability to learn new and innovative foraging tactics.

One dangerous predator along the coast of California easily outranks the sea otter in size, ferocity, and appetite, and that predator is the great white shark. Ten years ago, I went to Mexico's Isla Guadalupe, off the coast of Baja California, to cage dive with the white sharks that gather in the island's waters to prey on the resident northern elephant seals. On that assignment, I was focused on underwater critters and didn't notice the Pacific and common loons that occur around the island. A loon would be nothing more than an appetizing tidbit for a four-metre (13 ft.), 1,600 kilogram (3,527 lb.) white shark, but these consummate opportunists rarely pass up a meal. Indeed, the stomach contents of sharks caught off the coast of California include loons, but there is no record as to which shark species were involved.

CHAPTER 8

The Road Ahead

Some 500 years ago, the Italian genius Leonardo da Vinci wrote, "Human creatures will forever be fighting and killing one another. They will destroy the vast forests of the world and when they are filled with food they will deal out death, labour, terror and banishment to every living thing. Everything on earth, or under it, or in the waters will be pursued, disturbed or spoiled or removed from one country to another."

In the many books I have written about ecosystems and wildlife, I have tried, whenever possible, to avoid talking about threats. Not because the natural world is free from them, by any estimation, but because the topic of threats is so upsetting to tackle. Threats to wildlife and the environment certainly existed when I began writing about the natural world more than forty years ago, and the situation has only gotten worse. There is an elephant in the room, and it, above all else, will dictate the future of not only loons but the planet itself—and us with it. That elephant is unrestrained human population growth. It's the emotional topic no one wants to address. As of January 2022, the world population was roughly 7.9 billion people, and it is increasing every year by an additional 66 million. Add to this, the ever-shrinking area of habitable land on the planet because of desertification, rising sea levels, and recurrent lethal heat waves resulting from the incontestable consequences of climate change, and you have more people being squeezed into a smaller and smaller space. It's simple: we are a species out of control, driven as all organisms are by genetically programmed self-interest. But humans have an advantage over all other organisms. We have an immense brain that can logically evaluate simple facts, although our analysis is too often clouded by misplaced cultural priorities, racial prejudices, junk science, and bigoted religious beliefs. We direct our collective intelligence towards disease suppression and enhanced food production when so many challenges could be lessened if there were simply fewer of us crowding the planet. Some population ecologists estimate that the sustainable carrying capacity of Earth is no more than 3 billion hopeful inhabitants, especially if we value sharing the space with a modicum of biodiversity. Yet, here we sit with a congested 7.9 billion. Does any intelligent observer really think this is going to end well if we do not change direction immediately? Will Leonardo's 500-year-old prediction unfold while we and our sophisticated computers fiddle and fuss, ignoring the elephant in the room?

‹ *Opposite.* Even the most pristine-looking northern lake can be contaminated with acid and mercury, making it uninhabitable for nesting loons.

> *Opposite.* In Canada, in the early 1990s, pairs of common loons produced an average of 0.7 young per year. In recent years, this has fallen to about 0.55. When chick production falls below 0.48, the population can no longer sustain itself and it slowly declines.

Perhaps now you can understand why I always shy away from the topic of threats, because none of them can be meaningfully tackled unless we address the root problem—and that problem is us. We are the ones who spew carbon dioxide and methane into the atmosphere with reckless abandon, heating up the planet. We are the ones who dump chemical poisons into our waterways and oceans, disrupting endocrine systems and threatening the health of all. We are the ones who fell forests to feed extravagant urban sprawl, agriculture, infrastructure, and imprudent resource extraction. This is who we are, and this is a brief review of what we are doing to loons.

The International Union for Conservation of Nature (IUCN), which globally evaluates the status of species and the threats to them, currently designates four of the loons as species of Least Concern and the yellow-billed loon as Near Threatened. The designation is a rough estimation of the birds' global status, but despite the apparent rosiness of the reports, the IUCN cautions that not all is well with these northern birds.

Globally, both the red-throated loon and the Arctic loon are declining, but because of their large population size, vast range, and their slow rate of decline, they still fall within the organization's criteria for Least Concern. However, such a designation should be cautionary, recognizing that "least concern" does not mean no concern.

In 2021, Canadian researcher Kristin Bianchini and her coauthors reported that the country's common loon population, which comprises 94 percent of all nesting common loons, had steadily produced fewer surviving young over the last three decades—a combined consequence of acid rain, mercury pollution, climate warming, shoreline developments, and boating activity. Once again, because of the species' wide range and large population size, it falls within the IUCN's criteria for Least Concern despite these declines.

The yellow-billed loon, with a small global population of just 16,000 to 32,000 breeding birds, is suspected by the IUCN of undergoing a moderately rapid population decline due to unsustainable subsistence harvest. As a result, the yellow-bill is designated as Near Threatened.

The Pacific loon, with an estimated global population of 930,000 to 1.6 million, is the only loon believed to be increasing, and the only one that can safely be categorized as of Least Concern.

Despite my aversion to discussing threats to wildlife species, the discussion is a crucial one, and I will briefly review six of the major threats facing loons and their world: acid rain, mercury contamination, climate change, lead poisoning, oil spills, and human disturbance. Although every species of loon is at risk from these threats, most of the research has focused on the common loon on its breeding range in North America. As a result, the following discussion will reflect that limitation, although in many cases logical extrapolations of the risks can be made to the four other species of loons.

ACID RAIN

When I was a boy in the late 1950s and early '60s, my family and I often visited my aunt and uncle in the small town of Levack, Ontario, thirty-five kilometres (22 mi.) north of Sudbury, where my uncle worked in one of the local nickel mines. I always enjoyed the drive to their home, seeing the many crystalline lakes whose waters would sparkle like diamonds whenever a wind caressed their surfaces. Little did I know that many of the lakes I saw near Sudbury were slowly being killed by acid rain.

According to loon researcher Kristin Bianchini, metal mining and smelting began in Sudbury in the 1880s and peaked in the 1950s and 1960s. By the mid-1970s, more than 7,000 lakes in a 17,000 square kilometre (6,564 sq. mi.) area surrounding the city were acidified. The burning of fossil fuels generates emissions of sulphur dioxide and nitrogen oxide, which react with water in the atmosphere to produce acids that fall as acid rain, acid fog, acid sleet, and acid snow. In the 1960s, the Sudbury mines were one of the world's largest sources of these toxic emissions, releasing roughly 2.5 million metric tonnes (2.8 million tons) per year.

Scientists use the pH scale to determine whether a solution is acidic or alkaline. The scale ranges from 1 to 14. A neutral solution has a pH of 7; a value less than 7 is acidic, and a value greater than 7 is alkaline. Most drinking water has a neutral pH, whereas lemon juice has a pH of 3; vinegar, 4; toothpaste, 9; and oven cleaner, 13. Researchers naturally wondered what impact such acidity might have on nesting loons.

Working in the Sudbury area, Robert Alvo reported on thirty-eight lakes that were monitored for twenty-five years and discovered that fish populations stopped reproducing once the pH dipped below 5.5, eventually leading to the total elimination of fish. Furthermore, loons attempting to raise young on such lakes had to rely solely on invertebrates to feed their chicks. Once the pH dipped below 4.4, sensitive invertebrate populations also declined, and loon chicks could no longer be raised on these acidified lakes.

Acid contamination of lakes and forests is certainly not limited to North America. Worldwide, there has been an increasing demand for electricity. For example, since the year 2000, increasing levels of acid precipitation, sometimes with pH values less than 2.4, have been reported falling on areas downwind from industrial regions in China, Russia, and India, where electricity is being generated by the burning of sulphur-containing coal.

Alvo wondered if such damaging acid contamination of watersheds was reversible. His long-term study was able to explore this question. From the 1980s to the early 2000s, as sulphur dioxide emissions from the Sudbury smelters declined due to mitigation measures, the number of lakes with a pH less than 5 decreased from twenty-eight to six; this was accompanied by evidence that aquatic communities could recover. But the news was not all good. Despite the decline in acid contamination of Sudbury lakes, loon chick production in the lakes in the last forty years has continued to drop by 6.3 percent per year.

‹ *Opposite.* A pair of common ravens fly above a fog-shrouded forest in British Columbia. Acid rain is the popular term used to describe any form of precipitation that is acidic, including acid fog.

Researcher Kristin Bianchini suspects that factors other than acidification, including mercury contamination and/or climate change, may be implicated.

MERCURY CONTAMINATION

Mercury is a naturally occurring chemical element that leaches from bedrock into aquatic ecosystems. More worrisome than this natural source of mercury is the mercury-laden emissions spewed into the atmosphere from the burning of coal and the incineration of municipal waste—emissions that later settle in wetlands and contaminate them. Once in the water, bacteria convert the mercury into a dangerous biologically active form called methylmercury. This transformation is accelerated if the water is acidic and warm. As a result, the danger from mercury contamination is heightened if a watershed is subjected to acid rain and/or the increased water temperatures that result from global warming.

Once methylmercury is within an aquatic ecosystem, it accumulates in invertebrates and fish, and its concentration slowly increases as it moves higher up the food chain, with the highest concentrations being in the largest fish and in the birds that eat them. Biologists call this concentrating process *biomagnification*. Loons are predators at the top of their food chain. Since they consume large amounts of fish and live for several decades, they are uniquely positioned to accumulate high levels of methylmercury and suffer the toxic consequences. In some cases, the methylmercury concentration found in adult loons can be twenty-two times higher than in the fish they are eating. Loons are not completely defenceless in dealing with this toxic substance. They can store methylmercury in their liver and kidneys, and females can discard some of it in the eggs they lay. As well, large amounts of methylmercury are normally deposited in feathers, especially in flight feathers, so all loons can rid themselves of substantial amounts of the toxin each time they moult. The situation becomes problematic for loons when these natural excretory pathways for ridding the toxin from their bodies are insufficient to balance the mercury load they experience.

Researcher David Evers tested common loons for methylmercury levels in their feathers and blood in five regions of North America: Alaska, the Pacific Northwest, the Upper Great Lakes, New England, and Maritime Canada. The levels were lowest in Alaska and gradually increased eastward, reaching a peak in Maritime Canada, where they were more

> *Opposite.* Mercury is a neurotoxin that dramatically affects loon behaviour, including the commitment a pair has to incubating their eggs.

196

than five times higher than in Alaska. Evers blamed the industrial centres around the Great Lakes and the mid-Atlantic regions for polluting the waters. Evers also discovered that adult male common loons had much higher mercury levels than adult females. He attributed the difference to the fact that male loons are, on average, 21 percent heavier than females, and they prey on larger, older fish, which have higher levels of the toxin in their bodies.

Loons with high levels of methylmercury are lethargic and become what one researcher half-jokingly described as "bad parents." They spend less time incubating their eggs, feeding their chicks, and defending their territories. Furthermore, researcher Kristin Bianchini reported that mercury-contaminated eggs may fail to hatch; if they do hatch, the chicks have weaker immune systems, take fewer energy-saving rides on their parents' backs, and are less successful at evading predators. In the end, loon productivity declines and fewer chicks fledge. Methylmercury levels in some of the loons in the Upper Great Lakes, New England, and Maritime Canada are high enough to cause these adverse effects and may partially explain why these populations are declining.

^ *Above.* The polar bear has become the planet's "canary in the coal mine" alerting us to the consequences of global warming. The implications of climate change extend well beyond the melting Arctic pack ice and will impact virtually all life on Earth.

CLIMATE CHANGE

It's amazing how circumstances can change in a lifetime. In the 1970s, few people talked about climate change or global warming. Today, fifty years later, a warming planet is one of the greatest threats facing humanity, yet we seem collectively uncommitted to confront that reality. In November 2021, global leaders from 197 countries—minus those from two of the largest polluters on the planet, China and Russia—met in Glasgow, Scotland, for the United Nations climate change convention (COP26). The interests of the fossil fuel industry were on full display, with over 500 lobbyists promoting their cause, more than the delegates from any single country. Despite all the impassioned rhetoric and empty promises, the end result is,

according to a multitude of climate scientists, that Earth is still projected to warm by a devastating 2.4°C (4.3°F) by the end of this century. A simple fact is repeatedly ignored. You cannot negotiate with physics. Longtime climate activist Bill McKibben says it best: "Physics is an immature negotiator. It does what it wants, and we cannot change that." Humanity's only option is to understand and accept that fact—and work with it.

Biologist Allison Byrd predicts that climate change will cause a northward shift in the breeding range of many boreal avian species, including the common loon. Researcher Kyle McCarthy, studying in New Hampshire and Maine, suggested that in the next thirty years average May temperatures in New England may increase by nearly 2°C (3.6°F), with monthly highs possibly increasing by 3.4°C (6.1°F). At the same time, November averages could increase by 4°C (7.2°F), with highs increasing by up to 8.5°C (15.3°F). The increasing air temperature will be accompanied by extended periods of drought. The overall impact will include lowered water tables, sea level rises, habitat shifts, increased storm frequency and severity, and a mismatch between the timing of prey abundance and when loons raise their chicks and need a surplus of food.

In New Hampshire, in 2015, Chris Conrod evaluated the

impact of hot, wet weather on loon chick survival. In years when the total rainfall was five centimetres (2 in.) above average, state-wide loon chick survival rates fell by nearly 30 percent. Additionally, when average June-July temperatures exceeded 19°C (67°F), there was a similar reduction in loon chick survival. Climate models clearly project that both an increase in precipitation—particularly in extreme single events—as well as an increase in temperature will become the new norms for New England. By 2080, the Audubon Society predicts that the common loon will have lost 56 percent of its current summer range in the United States, and 75 percent of its winter range.

Researcher Kristin Bianchini and colleagues, reporting on forty years of common loon data in Canada, have a succinct warning: "Climate change could worsen the problems that acid rain and mercury pose for loons by intensifying changes in water levels and by raising water temperatures. Lower water during droughts exposes lake sediments to oxygen, which ... results in greater acidity when water levels rise again. Greater acidity, in turn, increases the activity of acid-loving, methylating bacteria, such that mercury also increases in fish and loons .... Furthermore, higher water temperatures ... also increase the activity of methylating bacteria, leading to even more mercury in fish and loons." They refer to this aggregate of ills as the "acid-mercury-climate hypothesis" and predict it will need to be the focus of conservation efforts if we hope to lessen the threats to loon survival.

Aside from the overall ecosystem impacts of climate change on Arctic sea ice and tundra, there has been virtually no research on how these changes will affect the survival of the other four species of loons.

LEAD POISONING

Lead poisoning in humans is a well-documented public health problem in many parts of the world. According to the World Health Organization (WHO), some of the lead originates in paint, glassware, ceramics, jewellery, toys, cosmetics, and traditional medicines. Drinking water carried through lead pipes or pipes joined with lead solder may also contain dangerous amounts of lead. The WHO warns: "At high levels of exposure, lead attacks the brain and central nervous system, causing coma, convulsions, and even death. Children who survive severe lead poisoning may be left with intellectual disability and behavioural disorders." Much less well-documented is the threat that lead poisoning poses to wildlife, and in particular, to waterfowl and loons.

The two most important sources of the lead impacting wildlife are from lead fishing tackle and lead shotgun pellets. In 1991, the United States finally banned the use of lead shotgun pellets, and seven years later, Canada did the same. In the decade preceding Canada's ban, the Canadian Wildlife Service, a federal government agency, estimated that 2,268 to 2,449 metric tonnes (2,500–2,700 tons) of lead per year were dumped into the environment from hunters and clay-target shooters. The lead leached into soils and wetlands where it broke down and slowly worked its way up the food chain. Anton Scheuhammer, the author of the Canadian Wildlife Service report, estimated that lead poisoning killed as many as 360,000 ducks and geese every year, and that another several million suffered sublethal poisoning.

In 2020, Gabriele Treu and colleagues reported on the lead shotgun pellet situation in the European Union. They estimated that more than 14,000 metric tonnes (15,432 tons) of lead pellets were scattered across the European environment annually. The use of lead in hunting ammunition is poorly regulated in the EU territory, and Treu concluded that upwards of 2 million birds die from lead poisoning every year.

Discarded and lost fishing tackle is another dangerous source of lead poisoning in wildlife, and unfortunately, it continues to be a problem. In Canada, the use of lead sinkers and jigs are partially restricted, but compliance by recreational anglers is less than 1 percent. About fifty metric tonnes (55 tons) of lead sinkers and jigs are manufactured in Canada each year, and an additional 465 metric tonnes (513 tons) are imported, the majority of which come from China, the United States, and Taiwan. A federal government website claims that every year the 3.3 million anglers in Canada will each purchase eleven to fifteen new sinkers and jigs to replace those that have been lost.

In the United States, the use of lead fishing tackle is banned in some states but not all. In Canada, lead sinker and jig ingestion has been documented in ten different wildlife species: the common loon, common merganser, herring gull, bald eagle, trumpeter swan, Canada goose, mallard, greater scaup, white-winged scoter, and snapping turtle. In the United States, twenty-three species have been afflicted, including white

> *Opposite.* This common loon has presumably swallowed a fish and the attached fishing line is now encircling its head and beak. There is no way to know if the tongue is entangled or damaged, or if the bird has swallowed a potentially lethal lead sinker. If there is a hook on the line and it reaches the acidic, grinding gizzard, it can be digested and not be an issue, but if it becomes lodged higher in the esophagus and penetrates major blood vessels, it can be fatal. Monofilament line itself is broken down relatively fast and seems to cause no clinical problems.

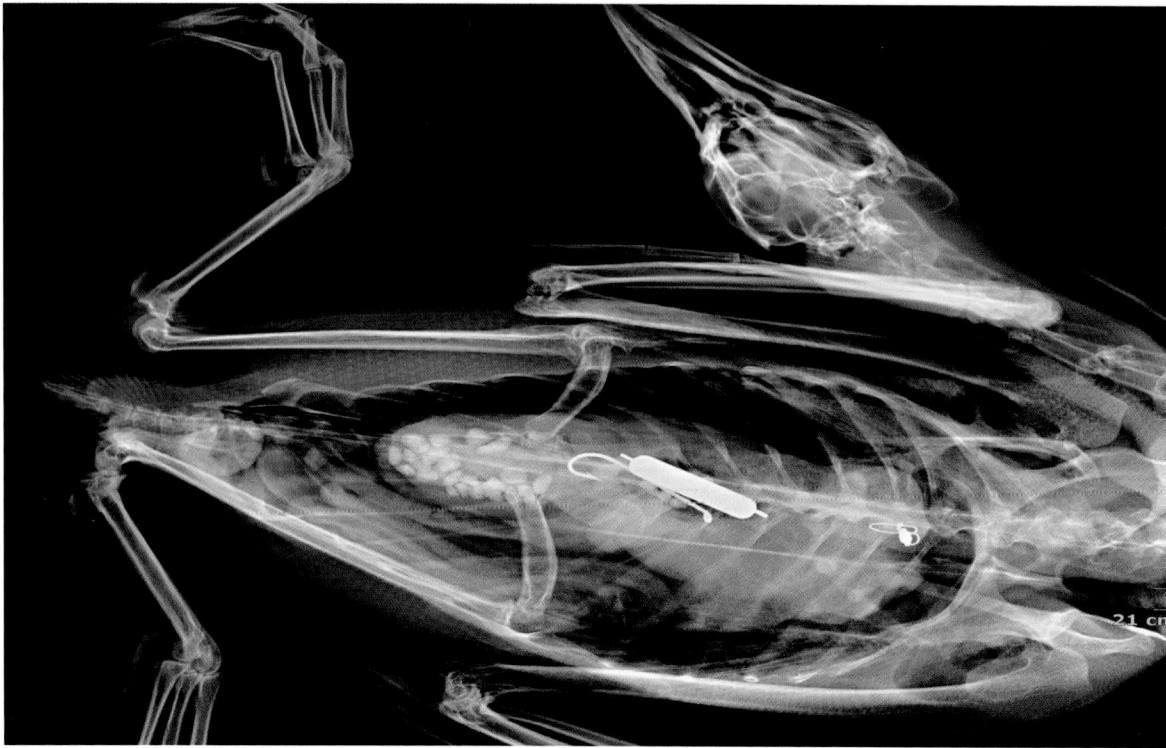

pelicans, sandhill cranes, white ibis, common and snowy egrets, and double-crested cormorants.

Of all the species impacted by the ingestion of lead fishing tackle, common loons sit at the top of the list. Lead poisoning is the cause of 10 to 50 percent of all adult common loon mortalities in North America, depending on location. In New England and eastern Canada, it is the number one cause of death. New Hampshire biologist Tiffany Grade and colleagues discovered that loons ingest the majority of lead tackle during the July-August summer period, when anglers are most active. This suggested that the loons were consuming lost bait fish with hooks, lines, and sinkers still attached to them, rather than scavenging lost tackle that had drifted to the bottoms of lakes. In 2018, writer Lauren

Chambliss, reporting for Cornell University, pointedly described the consequences of ingesting lead fishing tackle: "When a loon scoops up a leaded sinker or jig among the small rocks, the lead ends up in the gizzard, where it sends poison swimming through the loon's veins. Within days, the loon becomes lethargic and can't eat. Then paralysis sets in. Death eventually comes from a nasty combination of exposure, suffocation and starvation."

In both Canada and the United States, anglers often whine about the cost of replacing lead tackle with suitable substitutes made of steel, tin, brass, or polypropylene. The Canadian Wildlife Service estimates that these replacements actually raise the yearly fishing expenses of the average Canadian angler by a paltry 1 to 2 percent. I live in Alberta, and my response to anglers in the province is to just deal with it. Here is how I see it. In Alberta, there are 4.37 million residents, and the number of annual fishing licences issued in 2020 was 326,000, which translates into just 7 percent of the population. I don't want to stop people from fishing recreationally—as long as their impact doesn't affect the experience of the 93 percent of us who don't fish. That means, if you want to fish, then do it in a way that protects wildlife, or I and the majority of Albertans may justifiably vote to prohibit you from fishing at all. It's time anglers were made accountable for their consumptive use of the environment. I strongly suspect there are many other loon- and waterfowl-loving Canadian and US residents who might agree with this reasonable approach.

OIL SPILLS

A little over ten years ago, we all watched in horror as the damaged Deepwater Horizon oil rig spewed 795 million litres (210 million US gallons) of crude oil into the productive waters of the Gulf of Mexico. It was the largest marine oil spill in the history of the petroleum industry, and one of the largest environmental disasters in American history. During the five months it took to finally seal the hemorrhaging rig, we watched the shifting responsibility, the accountability battles, the unsuccessful containment efforts, the failure of dispersants, the suppression of the press, the coastlines swimming with oil, and the dead and dying wildlife victims. Roughly twenty years earlier, in 1989, we thought the Exxon Valdez oil tanker disaster was as bad as it could get. That catastrophe spilled 42 million litres (11 million US gallons) of crude oil into the pristine waters of Alaska's Prince William Sound and was a mere nineteenth the size of the Deepwater disaster. Researcher

Rebecca Field and colleagues reported that as many as 4,000 loons, including commons, Pacifics, red-throats, and yellow-bills, were lethally oiled in the Exxon Valdez disaster. Scientists estimate that for every oiled carcass they recover there are seven to nine other uncounted victims.

The threat from coastal oil spills continues today, despite the purported safeguards instituted by the petroleum industry. Most recently, in October 2021, the rupture of an underwater pipeline leaked 95,000 litres (25,000 US gallons) of crude oil onto the popular beaches of Southern California, igniting a heated discussion about phasing out offshore drilling along with other forms of oil extraction in the state. Oil industry specialists candidly admit there isn't a tanker, pipeline, or drill

∧ *Above.* The brown pelican is the state bird of Louisiana. This unfortunate bird was photographed on the coast of Louisiana where it had become completely soaked in oil and was unlikely to survive.

rig that will not eventually fail. It's not a question of if this happens again but when.

The port of Vancouver in British Columbia is Canada's largest, servicing upwards of fifty crude oil tankers every year, as well as over 3,000 cargo ships. Once the controversial Trans Mountain pipeline is completed in 2023, oil tanker traffic in Vancouver's offshore waters is predicted to increase eightfold to an estimated 400 tankers per year. Every spring, a million seabirds, including loons, shearwaters, phalaropes, and kittiwakes, head north to their summer nesting grounds, and many temporarily rest and feed in the offshore waters from Vancouver and nearby Vancouver Island. This area is also one of the world's key coastal locations where large numbers of northern seabirds, including loons, concentrate in winter. Even a relatively small oil spill could be devastating to the local seabird population should the spill occur in winter when bird numbers are at their peak.

Oil destroys the waterproof qualities of a bird's plumage by disrupting the feather arrangement, which predisposes the victim to hypothermia, especially during the chilly winter months. Canadian Wildlife Service biologists Kees and Rebecca

Vermeer reported that birds soiled with oil may lose their buoyancy and drown. Even if they make it to shore, they may ultimately die anyway. Such afflicted birds can clean half the oil from their feathers in the first week after oiling, ingesting most of it in the process. This can then lead to lethal liver and kidney damage, and severe inflammation of their intestinal tract.

At a loon conference in 1992, Rebecca Field and Michael North warned that yellow-billed loons, the rarest of the loon species, are especially at risk if an oil spill were to occur in coastal waters during winter. The authors felt that the loons were especially vulnerable because they overwinter in and migrate through coastal areas where spills are likely to occur. As well, the birds spend the bulk of their time on the water surface, especially when moulting in winter. With each dive, the oil is spread over their entire bodies. Additionally, the small fish they ingest would likely be contaminated with oil, adding a further risk. Although Field and North were focused on the threats to yellow-billed loons from a future oil spill, the four other loon species face the same dangers and for exactly the same reasons.

Loons are considered a species that is especially susceptible to the toxic effects of oil. Even those that don't die immediately

> *Opposite*. This oiled common loon had tried to clean its feathers, and the vigorous preening left its plumage dishevelled.

may suffer sublethal effects. In the first winter following the Deepwater Horizon spill, the oiling rates in common loons still ranged from 7 to 24 percent, which would have likely caused significant additional mortality over and above the loons that died during the months when the rig was still leaking.

Among the most dangerous components of spilled oil are polycyclic aromatic hydrocarbons (PAHs). These substances are extremely toxic to wildlife and humans. From 2011 to 2015, researcher James Paruk and colleagues tested the PAH levels in the blood of ninety-three common loons, including adults and subadults that were wintering in the Gulf of Mexico where they spend four to five months each year. Loons with the highest PAH levels were underweight. Paruk and his coauthors wondered if chronic levels of PAH in the environment might lead to a number of sublethal effects that could decrease the birds' survival. In winter, when they undergo a complete moult of their wing feathers, common loons require additional energy from their diet. If these birds are already underweight because of PAH contamination, the added stress of moulting may be too much for them to survive. Common loons wintering in the Gulf of Mexico also need to be in good condition to undertake their

long migration. The researchers concluded that oil pollution in the Gulf of Mexico may have a significant impact on migratory loons by reducing their future reproductive success. They emphasized the need for continued research to quantify potential long-term effects of chronic exposure to oil pollution.

HUMAN DISTURBANCE

Of all the threats facing loons, human disturbance is one that loons sometimes seem able to adjust to, provided humans also modify their behaviour. Loons can become habituated to people, but it takes time and may only occur if the breeding birds were themselves reared on a busy lake. Loons have individual personalities, like every group of wild birds and mammals with which I have worked. Some individuals are timid and easily disturbed while others are bold and bravely allow humans to approach them closely.

In Alaska's Kenai National Wildlife Refuge, one study compared the reaction of nesting common loons to canoeists on remote lakes versus those on well-travelled lakes. On the busy lakes, the resident loons would usually remain on their nests until the canoe approached within less than 8.5 metres

(28 ft.). On remote, rarely visited lakes, canoeists elicited a reaction from the loons at a distance of 113 metres (370 ft.). In a similar study in the well-paddled Boundary Waters Canoe Area of northern Minnesota, researchers James Titus and Larry VanDruff noted, as I did, that nesting common loons have different temperaments, and this is reflected in their response to canoeists. They called loons that were tolerant "stickers." They suspected that less tolerant birds simply moved to quieter lakes rather than be stressed by the constant parade of canoeists on the more popular lakes.

What about the disturbance caused by motorboats and cottages? During incubation, loons are sensitive to boats of any description. If boaters continue past a nesting loon without altering their progress or course, whether they are in a motorboat or a canoe, a loon will often remain on the nest. If boaters loiter to sightsee or fish, a loon will then often react adversely and leave its nest, signalling its annoyance with noisy tremolos, persistent penguin displays, and splash dives. As for cottages, it seems that it is not the buildings that matter to loons but the people moving around them. New Hampshire's Loon Preservation Committee reported that loons nesting on busy

> *Opposite.* This habituated pair of common loons in British Columbia nested on a lake with multiple cottages and summer homes, yet it successfully raised chicks almost every year.

lakes in their state were more successful when cottage owners delayed their summer arrival until loon chicks had hatched. Researcher Marianne Heimberger and colleagues studied common loons in the cottage country north of Toronto, Ontario. They found that hatching success declined as the number of cottages increased, but the reduction was less if the cottage was more than 150 metres (164 yd.) from the nest. Once the chicks hatched, parents usually moved them to a relatively quiet area of the lake where the likelihood of successfully raising them was the same as raising chicks on a lake with no human activity.

Common loons are not the only loon species disturbed by human activity. In Finland and Sweden, researchers found that cottages and/or boaters on lakes had a negative effect on nesting Arctic loons.

Today, on many busy lakes in North America, park officials and conservation groups install signs and protective barriers around the shoreline nests of common loons. These serve to alert the public to the birds' presence and caution them to temporarily stay away during the vulnerable incubation period. Such simple preventive measures significantly improve the reproductive success of the loons.

In 2020, the Loon Preservation Committee reported on a new recreational pressure, wakeboarding, in which the rider stands on a short board with foot bindings and is towed behind a fast-moving motorboat. The sport generates high-energy waves, twice the height of those produced in waterskiing. Researchers fear that such waves may increase shoreline erosion and inundate loon nests.

The threats facing loons are not limited to the six topics briefly discussed above. Loons also die in botulism outbreaks, drown in fishing nests, and are displaced from winter feeding areas by offshore wind farms. The five loon species inhabiting our northern lands are vital long-term biological indicators of the health of Arctic and temperate ecosystems, the same ecosystems that so many of us share. But more than that, the lives of loons, bears, alligators, owls, penguins, and so many of the other creatures about which I have written in the last fifty years keep me humble. They help me to see humanity for what it is, and to understand where I fit in the spectrum of life. We need to preserve these animals and their wilderness haunts for ourselves and for the dreams of future generations. We should fight for these things as if our lives depend on it, because they do.

Acknowledgments

I had been thinking about writing a book on loons for nearly fifty years, starting in the early 1970s when I used a photo blind for the first time and positioned it near a nesting common loon. Whenever I spend hours quietly hidden inside a blind, my mind invariably wanders, and I wonder whether I could expand the experience and develop it into a book. Most often, however, the thought is a fleeting one, merely a game I play with myself to pass the time. Nonetheless, the idea of a loon book kept surfacing over the decades, usually when I was photographing in the Arctic and had spent some time working with these handsome waterbirds. In March 2020, everything changed when a viral pandemic shut the Canadian borders, and all the wonderful ecotourism jobs I had lined up for the year evaporated overnight. There I was, stuck in Alberta in the midst of a global crisis, jobless, and with no plans for the months ahead. As Elbert Hubbard penned a hundred years ago, "When life gives you lemons, make lemonade." It was the perfect time to pour my heart into a book about loons while following the pandemic rules of social distancing and isolation. This book is my version of lemonade.

Like every book I have ever written, this project was greatly assisted by generous help from others. I am especially grateful for the conversations and advice given by the Alberta "nature nut" John Acorn, Nunavut fixer Vicki Aitoak, outdoor writer and photographer Michael Furtman, New Hampshire loon biologist Tiffany Grade, Alberta "loon-atic" Bonnie Grzesiak, wildlife biologist Kevin Kenow, veterinarian Dr. Mark Pokras, loon researcher Dr. Nina Schoch, biologist Samantha Stamler, ichthyologist Dr. Michael Sullivan, ecologist Scott Sutcliffe, and mathematician Peter Thompson.

Photographs add strength to every story, and although I took the lion's share of images in this book, I asked a few others for their help with imagery I thought would complement and enrich the text. Libby Libbey contributed a cringe-worthy photo of a nesting common loon being mercilessly tormented by blackflies. British Columbia photographer Doug Giles allowed me to choose two images from his wonderful rare photo coverage of a common loon adopting a goldeneye duckling. New Brunswick photographer Dave Lilly donated his superlative photograph of a wintering common loon feeding on a crab. Longtime friend, travel companion, and photographer Kathy Parker enthusiastically gave me one of the razor-sharp Arctic loon photos she took in Iceland.

^ *Above*: The author's wife, Aubrey Lang, often joined him on outings to observe and photograph nesting loons."

Others helped in unexpected ways. Gifted photographer Bob Cook was a frequent companion on loon photo ventures, and he graciously loaned me his rubber boat whenever I needed it. Polar ecologist Dr. Andrew Derocher made the pursuit of technical papers a simple matter of "ask, and ye shall receive." The speed and enthusiasm with which he did this is still a marvel to me. Veterinarian Dr. Dayna Goldsmith allowed me to photograph several loon necropsies and was patient with my tedious requests for "just one more shot." Biologist Brent Markham generously gave me three lightweight waterfowl decoys that I painted to resemble loons and used for photography. Warm and hospitable Alberta landowners Neil and Undine Maclaine gave me unlimited access to a private lake and a canoe, where I could observe common loons as I

never had before. Naturalist and photographer Jim Richards often advised me on my quest for yellow-billed loons and generously sent me a selection of his superb loon photographs, but unfortunately, I was unable to slot any of them into the book. Still, I thank him for his kind offer. And, finally, a trio of enthusiastic naturalists and photographers, Dr. Madeline Kalbach, Susan Stauffer, and Pat Wismer, repeatedly hired me to show them loons, and the funds from those outings helped to finance this project. I will always remember them as enthusiastic patrons of the book.

Once the book was written, I surrendered the text to four brave souls for technical review. It is a daunting task to carefully read an entire manuscript with enough attention to make constructive criticisms, and I am grateful to my reviewers for finding the time to undertake this valuable yet onerous job. My thanks go out to indefatigable Alaskan physician and self-described nature nerd Dr. Beth Baker, wildlife biologist Dr. Kristin Bianchini, premier loon researcher Dr. Walter Piper, and the friendly, untiring senior biologist of New Hampshire's Loon Preservation Committee, Harry Vogel. All were thorough and methodical in their reviews and insightful with their criticisms. Of course, I alone accept all responsibility for any errors that may have crept into the text.

This is my twenty-first book with Fitzhenry & Whiteside, and I was so pleased that Sharon Fitzhenry wanted to proceed with this project. Special thanks to Chief Operating Officer Holly Doll, editor Carrie Love, and designer Tanya Montini for helping my vision come to life. It is an uncommon joy to work with such a team.

Finally, I come to my amazing wife of forty-eight years, Aubrey Lang. She has edited every book I have ever written, and her ability to spot weaknesses in my logic and improve the text in ways I never imagined still astounds me. She is a marvel. Aubrey accompanied me on many of my trips to the Arctic to work with loons, and those adventures were always made so much more enjoyable by her effervescent spirit and warm, loving manner.

Dr. Wayne Lynch has been a full-time natural history writer and wildlife photographer for over 40 years. He is the author of over 65 books written for adults and children, a globally recognized photographer with images published in over 80 countries, and a popular guest lecturer.

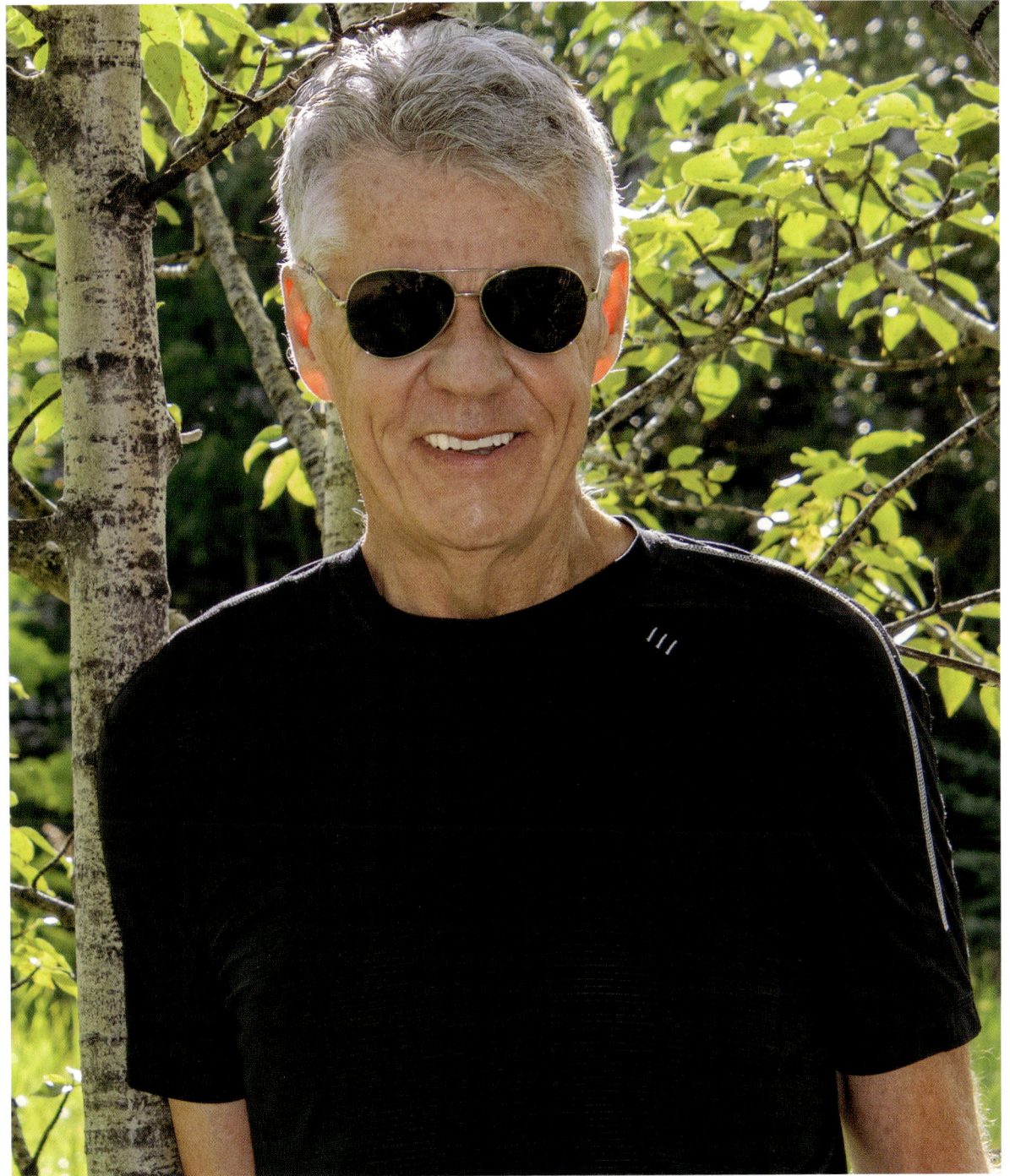

REFERENCES

GENERAL

Bent, A. C. (1919) 1963. *Life Histories of North America Diving Birds.* Dover Publications, New York, NY.

Birkhead, T. 2016. *The Most Perfect Thing: Inside (and outside) a Bird's Egg.* Bloomsbury, New York, NY.

Dregni, M., ed. 1996. *Loons: Song of the Wild.* Raincoast Books, Vancouver, BC.

Evers, D. C., and K. D. Taylor. 2014. *Journey with the Loon.* Willow Creek Press, Minocqua, WI.

Garthe, S., and O. Hüppop. 2004. Scaling possible adverse effects of marine wind farms on seabirds: developing and applying a vulnerability index. *J. Applied Ecology* 41:724–734.

Gaston, A. J. 2004. *Seabirds: A Natural History.* Yale University Press, New Haven, CT.

Hanson, T. 2011. *Feathers: The Evolution of a Natural Miracle.* Basic Books, New York, NY.

Hill, G. E. 2010. *Bird Coloration.* National Geographic Society, Washington, D.C.

Hutchinson, A. 1998. *Just Loons: A Wildlife Watcher's Guide.* Willow Creek Press, Minocqua, WI.

Johnsgard, P. A. 1987. *Diving Birds of North America.* University of Nebraska Press, Lincoln, NE.

Lang, A., and W. Lynch. 1989. *Loons.* Key Porter Books, Toronto, ON.

Lovette, I. J., and J. W. Fitzpatrick, eds. 2016. *Handbook of Bird Biology.* 3rd ed. Cornell Laboratory of Ornithology, Princeton University Press, Princeton, New Jersey.

Lynch, W. 2007. *Owls of the United States and Canada: A Complete Guide to Their Biology and Behavior.* Johns Hopkins University Press, Baltimore, MD.

Lynch, W. 2007. *Penguins of the World.* 2nd ed. Firefly Books, Richmond Hill, ON.

Martin, G. R. 2020. *Bird Senses: How and What Birds See, Hear, Smell, Taste, and Feel.* Pelagic Publishing, Exeter, UK.

Paruk, J. D. 2021. *Loon Lessons: Uncommon Encounters with the Great Northern Diver.* University of Minnesota Press, Minneapolis, MN.

Phillips, C. L. 1887. Egg-laying extraordinary in *Colaptes auratus. Auk* 4:346.

Rijke, A. M., and W. A. Jesser. 2011. The water penetration and repellency of feathers revisited. *Condor* 113(2):245–254.

Sibley, David Allen. 2000. *The Sibley Guide to Birds.* Alfred A. Knopf, New York, NY.

Smith, N. D. 2011. Body mass and foraging ecology predict evolutionary patterns of skeletal pneumaticity in the diverse "waterbird" clade. *Evolution* 66 (4):1059–1078.

Solovyeva, D. V., J. D. Paruk, J. Tash, et al. 2017. Post-breeding densities, population sizes and lake size partitioning of loon species in western Chukotka, Russia. *Contemporary Problems of Ecology* 10(6):621–631.

Soper, J. D. 1946. Ornithological results of the Baffin Island expeditions of 1928–1929 and 1930–1931, together with more recent records. *The Auk* 63(1):1-24.

Sprengelmeyer, Q. D. 2014. A phylogenetic reevaluation of the genus *Gavia* (Aves: Gaviiformes) using next-generation sequencing. MSc thesis, Northern Michigan University, Marquette, MI.

Todd, F. S. 1994. *10,001 Titillating Tidbits of Avian Trivia.* Ibis Publishing Company, Vista, CA.

Whitney, M. C., and D. A. Cristol. 2017. Impacts of sublethal mercury exposure on birds: a detailed review. In *Reviews of Environmental Contamination and Toxicology*, edited by P. de Voogt, vol. 244. Springer, Cham, Switzerland. https://doi.org/10.1007/398_2017_4.

Yang, T.-R., and P. M. Sander. 2018. The origin of the bird's beak: new insights from dinosaur incubation periods. *Biol. Lett.* 14:20180090. https://doi.org/10.1098/rsbl.2018.0090.

RED-THROATED LOON

Andres, B. A. 1993. Foraging flights of Pacific, *Gavia pacifica*, and red-throated, *G. stellata*, loons on Alaska's Coastal Plain. *Can. Field-Naturalist* 107(2):238–240.

Ball, J. R. 2004. Effects of parental provisioning and attendance on growth and survival of red-throated loon pre-fledglings: a potential mechanism linking marine regime shifts to population change. MSc thesis, Simon Fraser University, Burnaby, BC.

Bergman, R. D., and D. V. Derksen. 1977. Observations on Arctic and red-throated loons at Storkersen Point, Alaska. *Arctic* 30(1):41–51.

BirdLife International. 2018. *Gavia stellata. The IUCN Red List of Threatened Species* 2018:e.T22697829A131942584.

Davis, R. A. 1972. A comparative study of the use of habitat by Arctic loons and red-throated loons. PhD thesis, University of Western Ontario, London, ON.

Dickson, D. L. 1993. Breeding biology of red-throated loons in the Canadian Beaufort Sea region. *Arctic* 46(1):1–7.

Dickson, D. L. 1994. Nesting habitat of the red-throated loon, Gavia stellata, at Toker Point, Northwest Territories. *Can. Field-Naturalist* 108(1):10–16.

Duckworth, J., S. O'Brien, R. Väisänen, et al. 2020. First biologging of a foraging red-throated loon *Gavia stellata* shows shallow and efficient diving in freshwater environments. *Marine Ornithology* 48:17–22.

Eberl, C. 1993. Effect of food, predation and climate on selection of breeding location by red-throated loons (*Gavia stellata*) in the High Arctic. MSc thesis, University of Ottawa, Ottawa, ON.

Eberl, C., and J. Picman. 1993. Effect of nest-site location on reproductive success of red-throated loons (*Gavia stellata*). Auk 110(3):436–444.

Enquist, M. 1983. How do Arctic skuas *Stercorarius parasiticus* search for diver eggs? *Ornis Fennica* 60:83–85.

Eriksson, M. O. G. 1994. Susceptibility of freshwater acidification by two species of loon: red-throated diver (*Gavia stellata*) and Arctic loon (*G. arctica*) in southwest Sweden. *Hydrobiologia* 279:439–444.

Eriksson, M. O. G., D. Blomqvist, M. Hake, and O. C. Johansson. 1990. Parental feeding in the red-throated diver *Gavia stellata*. *Ibis* 132:1–13.

Eriksson, M. O. G., I. Johansson, and C.-G. Ahlgren. 1992. Levels of mercury in eggs of red-throated diver (*Gavia stellata*) and black-throated diver (*G. arctica*) in southwest Sweden. *Ornis Svecica* 2:29–36.

Gomersall, C. H. 1986. Breeding performance of the red-throated diver *Gavia stellata* in Shetland. *Holarctic Ecology* 9(4):277–284.

Grant, G. S. 1996. Near-shore feeding behavior of common and red-throated loons in Onslow Bay, North Carolina. *Journal of the Elisha Mitchell Scientific Society* 112(3):103–107.

Guse, N., S. Garthe, and B. Schirmeister. 2009. Diet of red-throated divers *Gavia stellata* reflects the seasonal availability of Atlantic herring *Clupea harengus* in the southwestern Baltic Sea. *J. Sea Research* 62:268–275.

Johnson, R. A., and H. S. Johnson. 1935. A study of the nesting and family life of the red-throated loon. *Wilson Bulletin* 47(2):97–103.

Kleinschmidt, B., C. Burger, M. Dorsch, et al. 2019. The diet of red-throated divers (*Gavia stellata*) in the German Bight (North Sea) analyzed using molecular diagnostics. *Marine Biology* 166:77. https://doi.org/10.1007/s00227-019-3523-3.

Lehtonen, E. 2016. Breeding site selection and breeding success in red-throated divers (*Gavia stellata*): implications for wind power development. MSc thesis, Uppsala University, Uppsala, Sweden.

McCloskey, S. E., B. D. Uher-Koch, J.A. Schmutz, and T. F. Fondell. 2018. International migration patterns of red-throated loons (*Gavia stellata*) from four breeding populations in Alaska. *PLoS ONE* 13(1): e0189954. https://doi.org/10.1371/journal.pone.0189954.

Mee, A. 1991. Black-throated diver attacking and killing red-throated diver. *Scottish Birds* 16:140.

Norberg, R. A., and U. M. Norberg. 1971. Take-off, landing, and flight speed during fishing flights of *Gavia stellata* (Pont). *Ornis Scand*. 2:55–67.

Norberg, R. A., and U. M. Norberg. 1976. Size of fish carried by flying red-throated divers *Gavia stellate* (Pont.) to nearly fledged young in nesting tarn. *Ornis Fennica* 53:92–95.

Nummi, P., V.-M. Väänänen, R. Pakarinen, and E. Pienmunne. 2013. The red-throated diver (*Gavia stellata*) in human-disturbed habitats—building up a local population with the aid of artificial rafts. *Ornis Fennica* 90:16–22.

Poessel, S. A., B. D. Uher-Koch, J. M. Pearce, et al. 2020. Movements and habitat use of loons for assessment of conservation buffer zones in the Arctic Coastal Plain of northern Alaska. *Global Ecology and Conservation* 22. https://doi.org/10.1016/j.gecco.2020.e00980.

Reimchen, T. E., and S. Douglas. 1984. Feeding schedule and daily food consumption in red-throated loons (*Gavia stellata*) over the prefledging period. *Auk* 101:593–599.

Rizzolo, D. J. 2017. Contrasting diet, growth, and energy provisioning in loons breeding sympatrically in the Arctic. PhD thesis, University of Alaska, Fairbanks, AK.

Rizzolo, D. J., C. E. Gray, J. A. Schmutz, et al. 2020. Red-throated loon (*Gavia stellata*), version 2.0. In *Birds of the World*, edited by P. G. Rodewald and B. K. Keeney. Cornell Lab of Ornithology, Ithaca, NY. https://doi.org/10.2173/bow.retloo.02.

Rizzolo, D. J., J. A. Schmutz, S. E. McCloskey, and T. F. Fondell. 2014. Factors influencing nest survival and productivity of red-throated loons (*Gavia stellata*) in Alaska. *Condor* 116:574–587.

Schamel, D., and D. M. Tracy. 1985. Replacement clutches in the red-throated loon. *J. Field Ornithol.* 56(3):282–283.

Sherony, D. F., B. M. Ewald, and S. Kelling. 2000. Inland migration of red-throated loons. *J. Field Ornithol.* 71(2):310–320.

PACIFIC AND ARCTIC LOONS

Abraham, K. F. 1978. Adoption of spectacled eiders by Arctic loons. Condor 80:339-340.

Andres, B. A. 1993. Foraging flights of Pacific, *Gavia pacifica*, and red-throated, *G. stellata*, loons on Alaska's Coastal Plain. *Can. Field-Naturalist* 107(2):238–240.

Bergman, R. D., and D. V. Derksen. 1977. Observations on Arctic and red-throated loons at Storkersen Point, Alaska. *Arctic* 30(1):41–51.

BirdLife International. 2018. *Gavia arctica. The IUCN Red List of Threatened Species* 2018:e.T22697834A132606505. http://dx.doi.org/10.2305/IUCN.UK.2018-2.RLTS.T22697834A132606505.en.

BirdLife International. 2018. *Gavia pacifica. The IUCN Red List of Threatened Species* 2018:e.T22697839A132607134. http://dx.doi.org/10.2305/IUCN.UK.2018-2.RLTS.T22697839A132607134.en.

Davis, R. A. 1972. A comparative study of the use of habitat by Arctic loons and red-throated loons. PhD thesis, University of Western Ontario, London, ON.

Dunker, H. 1973. Habitat selection and territory size of the black-throated diver, *Gavia arctica*, in south Norway. *Norw. J. Zool.* 22:15–29.

Dunker, H., and K. Elgmork. 1973. Nesting of the black-throated diver, *Gavia arctica*, in small bodies of water. *Norw. J. Zool.* 21:33–37.

Eriksson, M. O. G. 1994. Susceptibility of freshwater acidification by two species of loon: red-throated diver (*Gavia stellata*) and Arctic loon (*G. arctica*) in southwest Sweden. *Hydrobiologia* 279:439–444.

Eriksson, M. O. G., I. Johansson, and C.-G. Ahlgren. 1992. Levels of mercury in eggs of red-throated diver (*Gavia stellata*) and black-throated diver (*G. arctica*) in southwest Sweden. *Ornis Svecica* 2:29–36.

Götmark, F., R. Neergaard, and M. Åhlund. 1989. Nesting ecology and management of the Arctic loon in Sweden. *J. Wildl. Manage.* 53(4):1025–1031.

Hake, M., T. Dahlgren, M. Åhlund, et al. 2005. The impact of water level fluctuation on the breeding success of the black-throated diver *Gavia arctica* in south-west Sweden. *Ornis Fennica* 82:1–12.

Hancock, M. 2000. Artificial floating islands for nesting black-throated divers *Gavia arctica* in Scotland: construction, use and effect on breeding success. *Bird Study* 47(2):165–175. https://doi.org/10.1080/00063650009461172.

Hatler, D. F. 1974. Bald eagle preys upon Arctic loon. *Auk* 91(4):825–827.

Haynes, T. B., J. A. Schmutz, M. S. Lindbergh, et al. 2014. Occupancy of yellow-billed and Pacific loons: evidence for interspecific competition and habitat mediated co-occurrence. *J. Avian Biology* 45:001–009.

Haynes, T. B., J. A. Schmutz, M. S. Lindbergh, and A. E. Rosenberger. 2014. Risk of predation and weather events affect nest site selection by sympatric (*Gavia pacifica*) and yellow-billed (*Gavia adamsii*) loons in Arctic habitats. *Waterbirds* 37(Special Publication 1):16–25.

Jackson, D. 2003. Between-lake differences in the diet and provisioning behaviour of black-throated divers *Gavia arctica* breeding in Scotland. *Ibis* 145:30–44.

Jones, R. N., and M. Obbard. 1970. Canada goose killed by Arctic loon and subsequent pairing of its mate. *Auk* 87(2):370–371.

Lensink, C. J. 1967. Arctic loon predation on ducklings. *Murrelet* 48(2):41.

Mee, A. 1991. Black-throated diver attacking and killing red-throated diver. *Scottish Birds* 16:140.

Moon, J.-I., J.-G. Park, S. Hur, et al. 2018. Mitochondrial genome of the black-throated loon, *Gavia arctica* (Gaviiformes: Gaviidae): phylogeny and evolutionary history. *Mitochondrial DNA Part B: Resources* 3(2):586–587. https://doi.org/10.1080/23802359.2018.1473733.

Mudge, G. P., and T. R. Talbot. 1993. The breeding biology and causes of nest failure of Scottish black-throated divers *Gavia arctica*. Ibis 135:113–120.

Petersen, M. R. 1979. Nesting ecology of Arctic loons. *Wilson Bulletin* 91(4):608–617.

Petersen, M. R. 1989. Nesting biology of Pacific loons, *Gavia pacifica*, on the Yukon-Kuskokwim Delta, Alaska. *Can. Field-Naturalist* 103(2):265–269.

Polak, M., and M. Ciach. 2007. Behaviour of black-throated diver (*Gavia arctica*) and red-throated diver (*Gavia stellata*) during autumn migration stopover. *Ornis Svecica* 17:90-94.

Rizzolo, D. J. 2017. Contrasting diet, growth, and energy provisioning in loons breeding sympatrically in the Arctic. PhD thesis, University of Alaska, Fairbanks, AK.

Robertson, G. J. 1993. Interspecific killing in the Pacific loon. *Wilson Bulletin* 105(3):534–535.

Russell, R. W. 2020. Arctic loon (*Gavia arctica*), version 1.0. In *Birds of the World*, edited by S. M. Billerman. Cornell Lab of Ornithology, Ithaca, NY. https://doi.org/10.2173/bow.arcloo.01.

Russell, R. W. 2020. Pacific loon (*Gavia pacifica*), version 1.0. In *Birds of the World*, edited by P. G. Rodewald. Cornell Lab of Ornithology, Ithaca, NY. https://doi.org/10.2173/bow.pacloo.01.

Sealy, S. G. 1973. Interspecific feeding assemblages of marine birds off British Columbia. *Auk* 90:796–802.

Sjölander, S. 1977. Reproductive behaviour of the black-throated diver *Gavia arctica*. *Ornis Scandinavica* 9(1):51–65.

Uher-Koch, B. D., J. A. Schmutz, and K. G. Wright. 2015. Nest visits and capture events affect breeding success of yellow-billed and Pacific loons. *Condor* 117:121–129.

Uher-Koch, B. D., K. G. Wright, and J. A. Schmutz. 2019. The influence of chick production on territory retention in Arctic-breeding Pacific and yellow-billed loons. *Condor* 121:1–11.

Uher-Koch, B. D., K. G. Wright, H. R. Uher-Koch, and J. A. Schmutz. 2020. Effects of fish populations on Pacific loon (*Gavia pacifica*) and yellow-billed loon (*Gavia adamsii*) lake occupancy and chick production in northern Alaska. *Arctic* 73(4):450–460.

Vermeer, K. 1977. Some observations on Arctic loons, Brandt's cormorants, and Bonaparte's gulls at Active pass, British Columbia. *Murrelet* 58(2):45–47.

Vermeer, K., and R. Vermeer. 1975. Oil threat to birds in the Canadian West Coast. *Can. Field-Naturalist* 89(3):278–298.

COMMON LOONS

Alvo, R. 2009. Common loon, *Gavia immer*, breeding success in relation to lake pH and lake size over 25 years. *Can. Field-Naturalist* 123(2):146–156.

Alvo, R., D. J. T. Hussell, and M. Berrill. 1988. The breeding success of common loons (*Gavia immer*) in relation to alkalinity and other lake characteristics in Ontario. *Can. J. Zool.* 66:746–752.

Barr, J. F. 1973. Feeding biology of the common loon in oligotrophic lakes of the Canadian Shield. PhD thesis, University of Guelph, Guelph, ON.

Barr, J. F. 1986. Population dynamics of the common loon associated with mercury contaminated waters in northwestern Ontario. Canadian Wildlife Service, Occasional Papers No. 56., Ottawa, ON.

Bianchini, K., R. Alvo, D. C. Tozer, and M. L. Mallory. 2021. Late ice-off negatively influences breeding in common loons. *Northeastern Naturalist* 28(1)65–76.

Bianchini, K., R. Alvo, D. C. Tozer, and M. L. Mallory. 2021. The legacy of regional industrial activity: is loon productivity negatively affected by acid rain? *Biological Conservation* 255.108977. https://doi.org/10.1016/j.biocon.2021.108977.

Bianchini, K., D. C. Tozer, R. Alvo, et al. 2021. Canadian lakes loon survey: celebrating 40 years of conservation, research, and monitoring. Birds Canada, Port Rowan, ON. https://www.birdscanada.org/bird-science/canadian-lakes-loon-survey/.

BirdLife International. 2018. Gavia immer. *The IUCN Red List of Threatened Species* 2018:e.T22697842A132607418. http://dx.doi.org/10.2305/IUCN.UK.2018-2.RLTS.T22697842A132607418.en.

Black, T. L. 1976. Parent-chick behavior from hatching to 13 days old in the common loon (*Gavia immer*). Report, Lake Itasca Biology Session, University of Minnesota, St. Paul, MN.

Burgess, N. M., D. C. Evers, and J. D. Kaplan. 2005. Mercury and other contaminants in common loons breeding in Atlantic Canada. *Ecotoxicology* 14:241–252.

Byrd, A. 2013. Common loon (*Gavia immer*) biogeography and reproductive success in an era of climate change. MSc thesis, University of Maine, Orono, ME.

Campbell, W. R., M. I. Preston, L. M. Van Damme, et al. 2008. Featured species—common loon. *Wildlife Afield* 5(1):54-146.

Clifton, G. T., and A. A. Biewener. 2018. Foot-propelled swimming kinematics and turning strategies in common loons. *J. Experimental Biology* 221 jeb168831. https://doi.org/10.1242/jeb.168831.

Cooley, J. H., D. R. Harris, V. S. Johnson, and C. J. Martin. 2019. Influence of nesting bald eagles (*Haliaeetus leucocephalus*) on common loon (*Gavia immer*) occupancy and productivity in New Hampshire. *Wilson Journal of Ornithology* 131(2):329-338.

Croskery, P. R. 1988. Reoccupation of common loon, *Gavia immer*, territories following removal of the resident pair. *Canadian Field-Naturalist* 102(2):264-265.

Daub, B. C. 1989. Behavior of common loons in winter. *J. Field Ornithol.* 60(3):305-311.

Davies, D. M. 1949. Description of *Simulium euryadminiculum*, a new species of blackfly (Simuliidae: Diptera). *Canad.* Ent. 81(2):45-49.

Desorbo, C. M., K. M. Taylor, D. E. Kramar, et al. 2006. Reproductive advantages for common loons using rafts. *J. Wildl. Manange.* 71(4):1206-1213.

Dulin, G. S. 1988. Pre-fledging feeding behavior and sibling rivalry in the common loon (*Gavia immer*). MSc thesis, Central Michigan University, Mount Pleasant, MI.

Evers, D. C. 1994. Activity budgets of a marked common loon (Gavia immer) nesting population. *Hydrobiologia* 279:415-420.

Evers, D. C. 2007. Status assessment and conservation plan for the common loon (*Gavia immer*) in North America: BRI Report 2007-20. US Fish and Wildlife Service, Hadley, MA.

Evers, D. C., J. D. Kaplan, M. W. Meyer, et al. 1998. Geographic trend in mercury measured in common loon feathers and blood. *Environmental Toxicology and Chemistry* 17(2):173-183.

Evers, D. C., L. J. Savoy, C. R. Desorbo, et al. 2008. Adverse effects from environmental mercury loads on breeding common loons. *Ecotoxicology* 17:69-81.

Evers, D. C., K. M. Taylor, A. Major, et al. 2003. Common loon eggs as indicators of methylmercury availability in North America. *Ecotoxicology* 12:69-81.

Evers, D. C., K. A. Williams, M. W. Meyer, et al. 2011. Spatial gradients of methylmercury for breeding common loons in the Laurentian Great Lakes region. *Ecotoxicology* 20:1609-1625.

Field, M., and T. M. Gehring. 2015. Physical, human disturbance, and regional social factors influencing common loon occupancy and reproductive success. *Condor* 115:589-597.

Forrester, D. J., W. R. Davidson, R. E. Lange, et al. Winter mortality of common loons in Florida coastal waters. *J. Wildl. Diseases* 33(4):833-847.

Franson, J. C., S. C. Hansen, M. A. Pokras, and R. Miconi. 2001. Size characteristics of stones ingested by common loons. *Condor* 103:189-191.

Gier, H. T. 1952. The air sacs of the loon. *Auk* 69:40-49.

Grade, T. J., M. A. Pokras, E. M. Laflamme, and H. S. Vogel. 2018. Population-level effects of lead fishing tackle on common loons. *J. Wildl. Manage.* 82(1):155-164.

Grant, G. S. 1996. Near-shore feeding behavior of common and red-throated loons in Onslow Bay, North Carolina. *Journal of the Elisha Mitchell Scientific Society* 112(3):103-107.

Gray, C. E., J. D. Paruk, C. R. DeSorbo, et al. 2014. Body mass in common loons (*Gavia immer*) strongly associated with migration distance. *Waterbirds* 37(sp1):64-75.

Haney, J. C. 1990. Winter habitat of common loons on the continental shelf of the southeastern United States. *Wilson Bulletin* 102(2):253-263.

Heimberger, M., D. Euler, and J. Barr. 1983. The impact of cottage development on common loon reproductive success in central Ontario. *Wilson Bulletin* 95(3):431-439.

Higgins, A., M. A. Hartwick, and M. A. Pokras. Forthcoming. Sternal punctures in common loons (*Gavia immer*): gender and territorial aggression.

Jukkala, G., and W. Piper. 2015. Common loon parents defend chicks according to both value and vulnerability. *J. Avian Biology* 46:551-558.

Keller, W., J. Heneberry, and B. A. Edwards. 2019. Recovery of acidified Sudbury, Ontario, Canada, lakes: a multi-decade synthesis and update. *Environ.* Rev. 27: 1-16.

Kenow, K. P., D. Adams, N. Schoch, et al. 2009. Migration patterns and wintering range of common loons breeding in the northeastern United States. *Waterbirds* 32(2):234-247.

Kenow, K. P., S. C. Houdek, L. J. Fara, et al. 2018. Distribution and foraging patterns of common loons on Lake Michigan with implications for exposure to type E avian botulism. *J. Great Lakes Research* 44:497-513.

Kenow, K. P., M. W. Meyer, D. C. Evers, et al. 2002. Use of satellite telemetry to identify common loon migration routes, staging areas, and wintering range. *Waterbirds* 25(4):449-458.

Kirkham, I. R., and S. R. Johnson. 1988. Interspecific aggression in loons. *J. Field Ornithol.* 59(1):3-6.

Klein, T. 1985. *Loon Magic.* Paper Birch Press, Ashland, WI.

La, V. T. 2010. The vocal behaviour of common loons (*Gavia immer*): Signalling strategies & landscape scale communication. MSc thesis, University of Windsor, Windsor, ON. https://scholar.uwindsor.ca/etd/8274.

Long, D., and J. D. Paruk. 2014. Unusually large wintering flock of common loons foraging in the Gulf of Mexico. *Southeastern Naturalist* 13(4):N49-N51.

Lowther, J. K., and D. M. Wood. 1964. Specificity of the black fly, *Simulium euryadminiculum* Davies, toward its host, the common loon. *Canad.* Ent. 96:911-913.

Mager, J. N., and C. Walcott. 2014. Dynamics of an aggressive vocalization in the common loon (*Gavia immer*): a review. *Waterbirds* 37(sp1):37-46.

Mager, J. N., C. Walcott, and D. Evers. 2007. Macrogeographic variation in the body size and territorial vocalizations of male common loons (*Gavia immer*). *Waterbirds* 30(1):64-72.

Mager, J. N., C. Walcott, and W. H. Piper. 2007. Male common loons, *Gavia immer*, communicate body mass and condition through dominant frequencies of territorial yodels. *Animal Behaviour* 73:683-690.

Mager, J. N., C. Walcott, and W. H. Piper. 2008. Nest platforms increase aggressive behavior in common loons. *Naturwissenschaften* 95:141-147

Mager, J. N., C. Walcott, and W. H. Piper. 2010. Common loons can differentiate yodels of neighboring and non-neighboring conspecifics. *J. Field Ornithol.* 81(4):392-401.

Mager, J. N., C. Walcott, and W. H. Piper. 2012. Male common loons signal greater aggressive motivation by lengthening territorial yodels. *Wilson Journal of Ornithology* 124(1):73-80.

McCarthy, K. P. 2010. Evaluation of disturbance factors and their effect on breeding common loons at Lake Umbagog National Wildlife Refuge, New Hampshire and Maine. PhD thesis, University of Massachusetts, Amherst, MA.

McCarthy, K. P., S. DeStefano, and T. Laskowski. 2010. Bald eagle predation on common loon egg. *J. Raptor Res.* 44(3):249–251.

McIntyre, J. W. 1975. Biology and behavior of the common loon (*Gavia immer*) with reference to its adaptability in a man-altered environment. PhD thesis, University of Minnesota, St. Paul, MN.

McIntyre, J. W. 1978. Wintering behavior of common loons. *Auk* 95:396–403.

McIntyre, J. W. 1983. Nurseries: a consideration of habitat requirements during the early chick-rearing period in common loons. *J. Field Ornithol.* 54(3):247–253.

McIntyre, J. W. 1983. Pre-migratory behavior of common loons on the autumn staging grounds. *Wilson Bulletin* 95(1): 125–132.

McIntyre, J. W. 1988. *The Common Loon: Spirit of the Northern Lakes*. Fitzhenry & Whiteside, Markham, ON.

McIntyre, J. W. 1994. Loons in freshwater lakes. *In Aquatic Birds in the Trophic Web of Lakes*, edited by J. J. Kerekes, 393–413. Developments in *Hydrobiologia*, vol. 96. Springer, Dordrecht, Netherlands. https://doi.org/10.1007/978-94-011-1128-7_36.

Morton, M. L., and M. E. Pereyra. 2011. Additional data and perspectives on interspecific aggression in the common loon, *Gavia immer. Can. Field-Naturalist* 125(1):61–62.

Nocera, J. J., and N. M. Burgess. 2002. Diving schedules of common loons in varying environments. *Can. J. Zool.* 80:1643–1648.

Olson, S. T., and W. H. Marshall. 1952. *The Common Loon in Minnesota*. Minnesota Museum of Natural History, Occasional Papers Number 5. University of Minnesota Press, Minneapolis, MN.

Parker, K. E. 1988. Common loon reproduction and chick feeding on acidified lakes in the Adirondack Park, New York. *Can. J. Zool.* 66:804–810.

Paruk, J. D. 1999. Territorial takeover in common loons (*Gavia immer*). *Wilson Bulletin* 111(1):116–117.

Paruk, J. D. 2008. Nocturnal behavior of the common loon, *Gavia immer. Can. Field-Naturalist* 122(1):70–72.

Paruk, J. D. 2009. Function of the foot waggle. *Wilson Journal of Ornithology* 121(2):392–398.

Paruk, J. D., E. M. Adams, H. Uher-Koch, et al. 2016. Polycyclic aromatic hydrocarbons in blood related to lower body mass in common loons. *Science of the Total Environment* 565:360–368.

Paruk, J. D., M. D. Chickering, D. Long IV, et al. 2015. Winter site fidelity and winter movements in common loons (*Gavia immer*) across North America. *Condor* 117:485–493.

Paruk, J. D., D. C. Evers, J. W. McIntyre, et al. 2021. Common loon (*Gavia immer*), version 2.0. In *Birds of the World*, edited by P. G. Rodewald and B. K. Keeney. Cornell Lab of Ornithology, Ithaca, NY. https://doi.org/10.2173/bow.comloo.02.

Paruk, J. D., D. Long, S. L. Ford, and D. C. Evers. 2014. Common loons (*Gavia immer*) wintering off the Louisiana coast tracked to Saskatchewan during the breeding season. *Waterbirds* 37(sp1):47–52.

Paruk, J. D., D. Long, C. Perkins, et al. 2014. Polycyclic aromatic hydrocarbons detected in common loons (*Gavia immer*) wintering off coastal Louisiana. *Waterbirds* 37(Special Publication 1):85–93.

Paruk, J. D., J. N. Mager, and D. C. Evers. 2014. Introduction: an overview of loon research and conservation in North America. *Waterbirds* 37(Special Publication 1):1–5.

Paruk, J. D., D. Seanfield, and T. Mack. 1999. Bald eagle predation on common loon chick. *Wilson Bulletin* 111(1):115–116.

Paruk, J. D., I. J. Stenhouse, B. J. Sigel, et al. 2019. Oiling of American white pelicans, common loons, and northern gannets in the winter following the Deepwater Horizon (MC252) oil spill. *Environ Monit Assess* 191(Supp 4):817. https://doi.org/10.1007/s10661-019-7925-y.

Piper, W. H., K. M. Brunk, J. A. Flory, and M. W. Meyer. 2017. The long shadow of senescence: age impacts survival and territory defense in loons. *J. Avian Biology* 48:1962–1070.

Piper, W. H., K. M. Brunk, G. Jukkala, et al. 2018. Aging male loons make a terminal investment in territory defense. *Behavioral Ecology and Sociobiology* 72:95. https://doi.org/10.1007/s00265-018-2511-9.

Piper, W. H., D. C. Evers, M. W. Meyer, et al. 1997. Genetic monogamy in the common loon (*Gavia immer*). *Behav. Ecol. Sociobiol.* 41:25–31.

Piper, W. H., J. S. Grear, and M. W. Meyer. 2012. Juvenile survival in common loons *Gavia immer*: effects of natal lake size and pH. *J. Avian Biology* 43:280–288.

Piper, W. [H.], J. Mager, and C. Walcott. 2011. Marking loons, making progress. *American Scientist* 99:220–227.

Piper, W. H., J. N. Mager, C. Walcott, et al. 2015. Territory settlement in common loons: no footholds but age and assessment are important. *Animal Behaviour* 104:155–163.

Piper, W. H., K. B. Tischler, and A. Reinke. 2018. Common loons respond adaptively to a black fly that reduces nesting success. *Auk* 135:788–797.

Piper, W. H., C. Walcott, J. N. Mager, et al. 2006. Prospecting in a solitary breeder: chick production elicits territorial intrusions in common loons. *Behavioral Ecology* 17:881–888.

Piper, W. H., C. Walcott, J. N. Mager, and F. J. Spilker. 2008. Fatal battles in common loons: a preliminary analysis. *Animal Behaviour* 75:1109–1115.

Piper, W. H., C. Walcott, J. N. Mager, and F. J. Spilker. 2008. Nestsite selection by male loons leads to sex-biased site familiarity. *J. Animal Ecology* 77:205–210.

Pittman, J. A. 1953. Direct observation of the flight speed of the common loon. *Wilson Bulletin* 65(3):213.

Riedman, M. L., and J. A. Estes. 1988. Predation on seabirds by sea otters. *Can. J. Zool.* 66:1396–1402.

Rummel, L., and C. Goetzinger. 1975. The communication of intraspecific aggression in the common loon. *Auk* 92:333–346.

Scheuhammer, A. M. 2003. Lead fishing sinkers and jigs in Canada: review of their use and toxic impacts on wildlife. Canadian Wildlife Service, Occasional Papers No. 108. Ottawa, ON.

Scheuhammer, A. M., and S. L. Norris. 1995. A review of the environmental impacts of lead shotshell ammunition and lead fishing weights in Canada. Canadian Wildlife Service, Occasional Paper No. 88. Ottawa, ON.

Schoch, N., M. J. Glennon, D. C. Evers, et al. 2014. The impact of mercury exposure on the common loon (*Gavia immer*) population in the Adirondack Park New York. *Waterbirds* 37(Special Publication 1):133–146.

Sjölander, S., and G. Ågren. 1972. Reproductive behavior of the common loon. *Wilson Bulletin* 84(3):296–308.

Sperry, M. J. 1987. Common loon attacks on waterfowl. *J. Field Ornithol.* 58(2):201–205.

Spitzer, P. R. 1995. Common loon mortality in marine habitats. *Environ. Rev.* 3:223–229.

Strong, P. I. V., and J. A. Bissonette. 1987. Effects of nest-site loss on common loons (*Gavia immer*). *Canadian Field-Naturalist* 101(4):581–583.

Strong, P. I. V., J. A. Bissonette, and J. S. Fair. 1987. Reuse of nesting and nursery areas by common loons. *J. Wildl. Manage.* 51(1):123–127.

Strong, P. I. V., and L. Hunsicker. 1987. Sibling rivalry in common loon chicks. *Passenger Pigeon* 49(3):136–137.

Sutcliffe, S. 1982. Prolonged incubation behavior in common loons. *Wilson Bulletin* 94(3):361–362.

Tischler, K. B. 2011. Species conservation assessment for the common loon (*Gavia immer*) in the Upper Great Lakes. USDA Forest Service, Eastern Region, Hancock, MI.

Titus, J. R., and L. W. VanDruff. 1981. Response of the common loon to recreational pressure in the Boundary Waters Canoe Area of northeastern Minnesota. *Wildlife Monographs*, 9:3–59.

Tozer, D. C., C. M. Falconer, and D. S. Badzinski. 2013. Common loon reproductive success in Canada: the west is best but not for long. *Avian Conservation and Ecology* 8(1):1. http://dx.doi.org/10.5751/ACE-00569-080101.

Tozer, R. 1993. Interspecific aggression by common loons. *Ontario Birds* 11(1):2–5.

Treu, G., W. Drost, and F. Stock. 2020. An evaluation of the proposal to regulate lead hunting ammunition through the European Union's REACH regulation. *Environ. Sci. Eur.* 32:68. https://doi.org/10.1186/s12302-020-00345-2.

Vermeer, K. 1973. Some aspects of the breeding and mortality of common loons in east-central Alberta. *Can. Field-Naturalist* 87:403–408.

Vliestra, L. S., and J. D. Paruk. 1997. Predation attempts on incubating common loons, *Gavia immer*, and the significance of shoreline nesting. *Can. Field-Naturalist* 111(4):656–657.

Walcott, C., J. N. Mager, and W. Piper. 2006. Changing territories, changing tunes: male loons, *Gavia immer*, change their vocalizations when they change their territories. *Animal Behaviour* 71 (3):673–683.

Warren, W. W. 1885. *History of the Ojibways, Based upon Traditions and Oral Statements.* Minnesota Historical Society. St. Paul, MN.

Weinandt, M. L., M. Meyer, M. Strand, and A. R. Lindsay. 2012. Cues used by the black fly, *Simulium annulus*, for attraction to the common loon, *Gavia immer. J. Vector Ecology* 37(2):359–364.

Wentz, L. E. 1990. Aspects of the nocturnal vocal behavior of the common loon (Aves: *Gavia immer*). PhD thesis, Ohio State University, Columbus, OH.

Yonge, K. S. 1981. The breeding cycle and annual production of the common loon (*Gavia immer*) in the boreal forest region. MSc thesis, Department of Zoology, University of Manitoba, Winnipeg, MB.

BirdLife International. 2018. *Gavia adamsii. The IUCN Red List of Threatened Species* 2018: e.T22697847A132607949. http://dx.doi.org/10.2305/IUCN.UK.2018-2.RLTS.T22697847A132607949.en.

Evers, D. C., J. A. Schmutz, N. Basu, et al. 2014. Historic and contemporary mercury exposure and potential risk to yellow-billed loons (*Gavia adamsii*) breeding in Alaska and Canada. *Waterbirds* 37(Special Publication 1):147–159.

Field, R., M. R. North, and J. Wells. 1992. Nesting activity of the yellow-billed loon (*Gavia adamsii*) in northern Alaska. *The Loon and Its Ecosystem: Status, Management and Environmental Concerns*, 164-170. American Loon Conference Proceedings, Bar Harbor, ME.

Field, R., M. R. North, and J. Wells. 1993. Nesting activity of yellow-billed loons on the Colville River Delta, Alaska, after the Exxon Valdez oil spill. *Wilson Bulletin* 105(2):325–332.

Haynes, T. B., J. A. Schmutz, J. F. Bromaghin, et al. 2015. Diet of yellow-billed loons (*Gavia adamsii*) in Arctic lakes during the nesting season inferred from fatty acid analysis. *Polar Biology*. https://doi.org/10.1007/s00300-015-1690-3.

Haynes, T. B., J. A. Schmutz, M. S. Lindbergh, et al. 2014. Occupancy of yellow-billed and Pacific loons: evidence for interspecific competition and habitat mediated co-occurrence. *J. Avian Biology* 45:001–009.

Haynes, T. B., J. A. Schmutz, M. S. Lindbergh, and A. E. Rosenberger. 2014. Risk of predation and weather events affect nest site selection by sympatric (*Gavia pacifica*) and yellow-billed (*Gavia adamsii*) loons in Arctic habitats. *Waterbirds* 37(Special Publication 1):16–25.

Johnson, C. B., A. M. Wildman, A. K. Prichard, and C. L. Rea. 2019. Territory occupancy by breeding yellow-billed loons near oil development. *J. Wildl. Manage.* 83(2):410–425.

North, M. R., and M. R. Ryan. 1989. Characteristics of lakes and nest sites used by yellow-billed loons in Arctic Alaska. *J. Field Ornithol.* 60(3):296–304.

Sage, B. L. 1971. A study of white-billed divers in arctic Alaska. *British Birds* 64:519–524.

Schmutz, J. A., J. G. Wright, C. R. Desorbo, et al. 2014. Size and retention of breeding territories of yellow-billed loons (*Gavia adamsii*) in Alaska and Canada. *Waterbirds* 37(Special Publication 1):53–63.

Sjölander, S., and G. Ågren. 1976. Reproductive behavior of the yellow-billed loon, *Gavia adamsii. Condor* 78:454–463.

Uher-Koch, B. D., M. R. North, and J. A. Schmutz. 2020. Yellow-billed loon (*Gavia adamsii*), version 1.0. In *Birds of the World*, edited by S. M. Billerman. Cornell Lab of Ornithology, Ithaca, NY. https://doi.org/10.2173/bow.yebloo.01.

Uher-Koch, B. D., J. A. Schmutz, and K. G. Wright. 2015. Nest visits and capture events affect breeding success of yellow-billed and Pacific loons. *Condor* 117:121–129.

Uher-Koch, B. D., K. G. Wright, and J. A. Schmutz. 2019. The influence of chick production on territory retention in Arctic-breeding Pacific and yellow-billed loons. *Condor* 121:1–11.

Uher-Koch, B. D., K. G. Wright, H. R. Uher-Koch, and J. A. Schmutz. 2020. Effects of fish populations on Pacific loon (*Gavia pacifica*) and yellow-billed loon (*Gavia adamsii*) lake occupancy and chick production in northern Alaska. *Arctic* 73(4):450–460.

PHOTO CREDITS

Page 8: John James Audubon, Public Domain

Page 14: Royal Alberta Museum

Page 16: Harry Vogel, New Hampshire Loon Preservation Committee

Page 20: (*inset Hesperornis regalis*) Loozrboy, Wikimedia Commons

Page 52: Dr. Kathy Parker

Page 68: (*upper*) Colin Pennycuik; (*lower*) Daniel Ksepka, Bruce Museum

Page 77: Dr. Dayna Goldsmith, Faculty of Veterinary Medicine, University of Calgary

Page 115: Nicolas Perrault, Wikimedia Commons

Page 117: Libby Libbey

Page 136: Dr. Mark Pokras, Faculty of Veterinary Medicine, Tufts University

Page 154: (*top and bottom*) Doug Giles

Page 175: Peter Massas, Wikimedia Commons

Page 181: (*map inset*) Courtesy of US Geological Survey, Public Domain

Page 185: Dave Lilly

Page 202: Dr. Mark Pokras, Faculty of Veterinary Medicine, Tufts University

Page 203: Louisiana GOHSEP, Wikimedia Commons

INDEX